"*The Sponsor Effect* demonstrates that investing in junior talent not only benefits the organization, it pays off for the sponsor. In fact, being an effective and prolific sponsor may well be a prerequisite to great success for leaders."

—**PETER CAPPELLI,** George W. Taylor Professor of Management, The Wharton School

"Sponsorship is not all about the protégé. Sponsors benefit as well. Sylvia Ann Hewlett provides convincing evidence that it pays off to be generous and supportive of young leaders. While you rise, they rise—and while they rise, you rise too."

—**KATHERINE PHILLIPS,** Reuben Mark Professor of Organizational Character, Columbia Business School

"Sylvia Ann Hewlett shows us, in no uncertain terms, what sponsorship is and how to make it work. *The Sponsor Effect* is a powerful tool, not only for executives trying to build their own careers, but for anyone hoping to make the workplace better, fairer, and more productive."

—**DEBORA SPAR,** Baker Foundation Professor, Harvard Business School

THE
SPONSOR
EFFECT

THE
SPONSOR
EFFECT

---•---

HOW TO BE A BETTER LEADER
BY INVESTING IN OTHERS

SYLVIA ANN HEWLETT

Harvard Business Review Press
Boston, Massachusetts

Library of Congress Cataloging-in-Publication data
    Names: Hewlett, Sylvia Ann, 1946- author.
    Title: The sponsor effect : how to be a better leader by investing in others
      / Sylvia Ann Hewlett.
    Description: Boston, Massachusetts : Harvard Business Review Press, [2019]
    Identifiers: LCCN 2018051111 | ISBN 9781633695658 (hardcover)
    Subjects: LCSH: Mentoring in business. | Leadership.
    Classification: LCC HF5385.H49 2019 | DDC 658.4/092--dc23 LC record
    available at https://lccn.loc.gov/2018051111
    ISBN: 978-1-63369-565-8
    eISBN: 978-1-63369-566-5

For my beloved husband, Richard, who helped me heal in 2018
and made me strong again

Contents

Part One

---•---

WHAT EVERY LEADER NEEDS TO KNOW

1

Sponsorship and the Power of Protégés

Who's delivering for you? Who has your back? Who's burnishing your brand? Who's expanding what you can get done in this world? Do you have loyal lieutenants who extend your reach?

If the answer to any of these questions is *no* or *I'm not sure*, then you're stacking the odds against yourself—whether you want to rise to the top of your organization or expand what you can do once you're there.

Consider basketball superstar LeBron James. Like many athletic stars, he has a few old friends who have accompanied him on his rise to fame. But unlike many stars, he didn't just hand out money to his old buddies. He sent them to school and steered them to internships where they strengthened their management and marketing skills—skills that he didn't have himself. His old friend Rich Paul, for example, now has his own talent agency, and another friend, Maverick

Carter, runs a production company. Paul, Carter, and the rest of James's inner circle have more than repaid the money he spent on them. In 2016, for example, Carter secured an endorsement deal for James with Nike that will, over time, be worth $1 billion.[1]

What sets LeBron James apart from so many athletic stars—and so many corporate leaders—was that he had the foresight to *invest* in the smart people he found. He didn't just keep in touch and write a few checks. He became a *sponsor*, powering up his talented friends with education and access. He helped them become high-performing, loyal protégés who could do for him what he couldn't do for himself: find and develop lucrative business opportunities that will ensure that he remains a successful and influential man long after he leaves the basketball court.

What Sponsorship Is—and Why You Should Care

Successful men and women understand that no matter how brilliant and driven they are, their time and energy are finite. They can't do it all. Every current leader or emerging star needs people around them who can increase their bandwidth, have their back, and provide a substantial value add, as Maverick Carter did when he produced that ten-figure endorsement contract for LeBron James.

Sponsorship is what enables this kind of opportunity. Sponsorship is a professional relationship in which an established or rising leader identifies and chooses an outstanding junior talent, develops that person's career, and reaps significant rewards for these efforts. As a mutually beneficial relationship, sponsorship is much deeper and more rewarding than traditional mentorship, a relationship in which a senior person "pays it forward" by giving guidance to someone more junior, often casually and for not very long.

Sponsorship relationships, on the other hand, require a commitment and an investment—for both sponsor and protégé. The sponsor must devote serious attention to identifying top junior talent, developing their skills, scrutinizing their progress, and advocating on their behalf. Protégés must deliver for their sponsor with stellar performance, rock-solid trustworthiness, and a differentiated skill set that adds value to the team and the organization, as well as to the individual sponsor.

Sponsorship thus isn't charity or granting a favor; it's a powerful leadership capability. Are you an entry- or mid-level manager, hoping to work better, grow your influence, and get promoted faster? The right protégé can fill gaps in your skill set, take responsibilities off your plate when your calendar gets crowded, offer moral support when you need it, and build your personal brand. Are you at the top of your organization or near it, seeking loyal lieutenants and the capacity to extend your reach throughout the enterprise? The right protégé will complement your leadership skills and style, provide honest feedback, make you feel that you have extra hours in the day, and enable your influence to persist even after you've moved on to your next role or opportunity.

If you're at the top, you may know the benefits of sponsorship already: leaders who rise to senior levels of their organization have almost always invested heavily in a select group of outstanding protégés who boost their productivity and become the next generation of the organization. But if you're not actively looking for these individuals, now is the time to start.

The Center for Talent Innovation (CTI), the think tank that I founded, recently conducted a nationally representative survey of full-time employees in white-collar jobs, ranging from entry-level professionals to C-suite executives. To cite just one sample from the data we collected, which I'll present throughout this book: for men, 38 percent of those with protégés report receiving a promotion in the last two years, compared to 22 percent of those without. That's a percent increase of 73 percent. For women, the difference is 27 percent versus 18 percent, or a 50 percent sponsor effect.[2]

For protégés, the data is equally telling. In my 2013 book, *Forget a Mentor, Find a Sponsor: The New Way to Fast-Track Your Career*, I quantified the value to protégés of winning a sponsor: male employees with a sponsor are 23 percent more likely to get that next promotion than those without. For female employees the figure is 19 percent.[3] In subsequent research, I showed that this benefit crosses geography and culture as well as gender. Employees at multinational companies get a particularly big bump when they earn sponsorship.

But how do protégés and sponsors give each other so much value?

As figure 1-1 illustrates, sponsorship is a two-way street and an investment: both parties put in effort and have skin in the game. As stated earlier, protégés provide multiple benefits for their sponsors; but sponsors also deliver for their protégés—believing in them and using up precious political capital for them, advocating for them, and providing them with "air cover" to take the risks that success often demands.

FIGURE 1-1 SPONSORSHIP IN ACTION

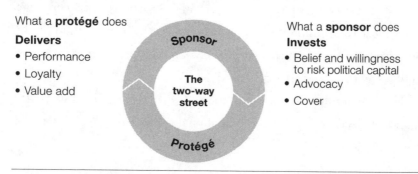

What a **protégé** does
Delivers
• Performance
• Loyalty
• Value add

Sponsor

The two-way street

Protégé

What a **sponsor** does
Invests
• Belief and willingness to risk political capital
• Advocacy
• Cover

Unlike a mentorship relationship, a sponsorship relationship places both the sponsor and the protégé in the position of actively and publicly *working* for each other's success.

That mutual commitment and effort (although, as we'll see, the protégé needs to do most of the work) leads to a relationship that boosts both parties. Consider the example of Larry Summers, eminent economist and former US Treasury Secretary, and Facebook COO Sheryl Sandberg. In 1990, when Sandberg was just a junior at Harvard, Summers—then a respected professor, but not well known outside his field—recognized Sandberg's value, believed in her potential, and singled her out for opportunities. She followed him to the World Bank as a research associate and then to the Treasury, where he made her his chief of staff. He then opened doors for her in the business world.

Sandberg certainly benefited from this relationship, but Summers did too. At first, she showed her value by being an enormously competent number two, but after she struck out on her own, her support of him remained unwavering. Years later when Summers made some ill-considered remarks about women, stating that they weren't equipped to succeed in STEM fields, Sandberg used her megaphone as a successful female executive to defend him as a man highly supportive of women—and she spoke up for him again and again.[4]

Sponsorship's reciprocity sets it apart not only from mentorship; it also sets it apart from standard corporate leadership development. Sponsors aren't just grooming someone to rise higher. They certainly are looking to fill organizational needs, but they're also taking a bet that their own careers can benefit if they invest in a promising individual's talent, skill sets, and trustworthiness. The ability to be an effective sponsor is a competency that can make the sponsor a better leader, both in the short term—with a value add and a boost to productivity—and in the medium and long terms, through bonds of loyalty and trust.

When Mellody Hobson, for example, started at Ariel Investments, she was just an intern, fresh out of college. Fiercely ambitious and hardworking, she soon attracted the attention of John Rogers, the chairman and CEO. Seeing her chance, she ramped up her energies to earn his serious support. In an interview, she told me that she became Rogers's "grasshopper," jumping and leaping to his every need.

Startled by her word choice, I asked her to dig deeper. What exactly did she do? Hobson hesitated, but after some thought she described learning to anticipate Rogers's wants, protect his time, and leverage his energies—making him a more effective leader and rainmaker. She also made it her business to feed him new marketing ideas. She was particularly creative in figuring out how to better reach African American women—a natural target for Rogers's firm. Her success in opening up this market has boosted the growth of the firm over many years.

Hobson is emphatic: her extraordinary commitment to Rogers is based on more than appreciation and promotions. He inspired her. She was and is a huge fan of his vision and what he has created at Ariel Investments. In her words, "It was easy to get totally vested in the mission of the most successful minority-owned investment company in America."

Hobson delivered for Rogers and he delivered for her: by age thirty-one she had become president of the firm, a title she holds to this day.

So protégés help sponsors, and sponsors return the favor. The reciprocal relationship should help both sponsor and protégé build a ladder to the top—and then thrive once there. But success demands that as a prospective sponsor you find the right people and take the right measures to help them become stellar protégés.

That requires a strategy for identifying talent, and this strategy should include people who are different from you and who can fill in some of your gaps. It often requires inspiring them to deliver over the long run for you and your organization; instructing them in skills (especially soft ones) that they lack; inspecting them to make sure they're living up to potential; and then instigating an explicit deal before you finally go full throttle on your investment in them.

This book offers a playbook to build this potent relationship and discover extraordinary payoffs. Sponsorship at its best is a long-term investment whose benefits keep compounding over the years and decades.

The Risks of Sponsorship

The flip side of sponsorship's power is a certain level of *risk*. In mentorship, if your mentee disappoints, no one holds you responsible; few may even know about the relationship. But what happens if your protégé, in whom you've publicly invested time, responsibilities, and reputational capital, disappoints? Maybe he or she, when push comes to shove, can't grow the bottom line, impress important stakeholders, or take work off your shoulders. Your own productivity and brand could take a hit.

And here's an even bigger risk: What if your protégé, who thanks to you has gained some power, turns on you and betrays your trust? That could threaten your own success and even your role in the organization.

Given this risk, as well as the enormous potential benefits, protégés need to *earn* a sponsor. To put it bluntly, no one will take on a protégé unless that protégé has clearly demonstrated their potential worth and *loyalty*. Sponsors, for their part, must devote effort and energy to identifying, including, inspiring, instructing, and inspecting a potential protégé *before* they instigate a deal and fully invest their precious clout and capital.

Consider what is perhaps the ultimate instance of sponsorship: a presidential candidate choosing a vice president for the ticket. This rides on trust, but also on a deep belief that your pick can deliver performance, loyalty, and a value add.

During the campaign, the vice presidential candidate must help the man or woman at the top of the ticket win: by acting as an effective proxy in debates and on the stump (performance); by bridging the party's ideological divides or providing geographical diversity (a value add); and by always deferring to the opinions and needs of the presidential candidate (loyalty).

Should the candidate win the stakes rise dramatically, as the vice president will be in the spotlight and have access to enormously sensitive information. Most critically, he or she will be a heartbeat away from the top job itself.

But in 2008, in his run for the presidency, the late senator John McCain chose a woman he hardly knew, Sarah Palin, as his running mate. Palin proved anything but loyal, likely damaged his campaign, and is now widely seen as a blemish on his legacy. That's what can happen when a sponsor fails to choose and develop a protégé correctly.

By contrast, consider the benefits that President George W. Bush drew from his relationship with Condoleezza Rice. Bush's father introduced him to Rice in 1998, as he was gearing up to run for the presidency. In the coming years, as she and George W. Bush bonded and he made her his protégé, she became his most trusted foreign policy adviser and perhaps his most trusted adviser, period. In a White House full—as every White House is—of men and women with their own personal agendas, Bush knew that Rice had only one agenda: his. "We are completely in sync," Bush told a gathering of diplomats when Rice was secretary of state. "When she speaks, you know that she is speaking for me."[5] Besides boosting Bush's foreign policy chops, Rice also helped create one component of his legacy that even his political foes have praised: his aid to Africa.[6]

A protégé's role in establishing a legacy is powerful in the business world too—and it applies whether you're retiring after rising to a high level in the organization, or moving on to new opportunities while your protégés stay with your former employer. Later in this book, I'll show just how powerful this legacy payoff can be. Whether it's Steve Howe, the US chairman and managing partner of professional services giant EY, handing off the baton to his longtime protégé; Steve Jobs ensuring that Apple would have sound leadership after his death; or an economist who vaulted to fame in 1919 extending his influence into our own day, sponsorship is the key to perpetuating your vision.

Sponsorship in Practice

Throughout this book, I show—through hard data and real-world examples, including interviews with several sitting CEOs—how sponsorship works in practice, how it can benefit you and the organization, how to maximize this investment's value, how to avoid common dangers, and how to make the benefits last. This book is not only grounded in CTI survey data, which shows how different tools and tactics have (or have not) worked for a broad swath of sponsors; it also features in-depth narratives, based on one-on-one interviews with sponsor-protégé pairs who share their experiences. Through these stories and conversations, you'll be able to see how each of these leaders found their protégés and developed the close relationships that opened up their organizations to new opportunities, broadened their individual sphere of influence, and perpetuated their vision.

Chapter 2 describes the essential properties of sponsorship, alongside data on the key benefits to sponsors. It also describes in detail common mistakes that keep sponsors from fully realizing the benefits of this relationship.

Chapter 3 zeroes in on some of the specific payoffs that sponsorship provides. As we'll see, protégés can enormously enhance their sponsors' reach and productivity, allowing them to progress further and faster. To illustrate how sponsorship can transform careers in every sector of the economy, I draw on examples from financial services, the media, Hollywood, and technology.

Part 2, the heart of this book, is a multi-step playbook for sponsors, as outlined in the sidebar, "Seven Steps to Effective Sponsorship." Understanding the details of each step in this playbook is crucial not just for maximizing value, but also for mitigating risks. If you're going to sponsor someone—linking their career to yours—they're going to be walking around with your brand on their forehead. How do you contain risk? What tools and tactics work best? How do you take these steps toward practical action? Each chapter in this section offers answers—summed up in how-to sections at the end of each step—based on data from our survey and tales from the trenches: the shared experiences of leaders who have succeeded in building sponsorship relationships that boost their careers and organizations.

Seven Steps to Effective Sponsorship

Step 1: Identify potential protégés. Know what to look for in the talent you're considering sponsoring, starting with performance and loyalty.

Step 2: Include diverse perspectives. Find those who are different from you—in their mindset and viewpoints, or in their gender, age, ethnicity, experience, or background.

Step 3: Inspire for performance and loyalty. Ensure that your protégés' values align with yours, and use their passion and ambition to spur them forward.

Step 4: Instruct to fill skill gaps. Work with your protégés to develop where they need to grow, whether that's in knowledge or soft skills.

Step 5: Inspect your prospects. Keep an eye on your protégés to ensure that they're continuing to deliver performance and also, most importantly, on the trustworthiness front.

Step 6: Instigate a deal. Having inspired, instructed, and inspected, now make the ask, specifying in some detail the two-way flow of value.

Step 7: Invest in three ways. You now need to be "all in." Commit your political capital and your clout, while providing air cover so that your protégés can take risks.

Seven steps may sound like a serious expenditure of time—and time is the last thing that most readers of this book have to spare. But when done right, sponsors find that they can align the balance of investment and reward in their favor from the start. For example, sponsorship immediately increases your bandwidth since a well-chosen protégé will take over some of your more onerous work tasks, freeing up your time for your highest priorities.

The final section of the playbook puts all seven steps together by featuring one-on-one interviews with leaders from EY, one of the world's biggest professional services firms. The voices of four EY sponsor-protégé pairs allow the reader to appreciate how this highly reciprocal relationship works at a concrete, granular level for managers at the midpoint in their careers, as well as those at the top of the ladder. These voices also demonstrate how sponsorship cascades through an organization, as others see the value of both earning sponsorship and developing protégés themselves.

In part 3, we shift the discussion to two additional pieces of the sponsorship puzzle: the potential trip wire of sexual relationships (and related fears) and the potential boon of a long-term legacy. Chapter 12 offers a guide to sponsorship in the age of #MeToo, a movement that has led not only to focused and valuable attention to an ancient problem, but also to new anxieties. It is important to have sponsorship relationships cross the lines of gender and generation, otherwise many highly qualified employees stall out in midcareer, or take their skills and energies elsewhere. But many leaders are hesitant to align themselves too closely with someone of the opposite sex because of gossip and risk. In this chapter I show how to avoid any hint of impropriety while building the bonds that sponsorship requires. With a few simple steps, men and women can create respect-filled spaces to sponsor one another without any danger to careers, reputations, or the organizations they work for.

Chapter 13 concludes the book with a look at how sponsorship—which helped you move up the ladder—can deepen your legacy going forward. Whether you're a CEO looking to find a successor, or a middle-level manager shifting roles, you'll want the person who fills your shoes to value your contribution and honor your vision long after you've gone. This chapter provides data on the impact of sponsorship on reputation going forward. It also provides vivid examples of how legacy can shine—or falter—based on the strength of a sponsor-protégé relationship.

From start to finish, sponsorship is a rich journey, one that will transform how you look at the talent that surrounds you—and your own career. Let's get started.

2

Presenting the Research—and Common Mistakes

Sponsorship is a long-term, active, and *reciprocal* investment. You're not "paying it forward" by helping out someone younger. Nor are you exploiting their talents and energy without giving anything in return. As a sponsor, you're providing behind-the-scenes support, active advocacy, and air cover; your protégé gives you performance and ability, loyalty and commitment, and (if you make an effort to include the right talent) a special value add with skills you don't have.

CTI data, some of which I'll present in this chapter, shows the benefits of sponsorship, as well as the common mistakes that sponsors make. Some of these mistakes occur because, even though many successful business leaders grasp sponsorship's value, their understanding is often merely intuitive. They act from instinct, not from a road map.

It is worthwhile to take a look at how sponsorship works in a field where it is both highly traditional and utterly explicit: politics. Precisely the same model, as we'll see later, applies to the business world, academia, and beyond.

Politicians Know Sponsorship

How clear-cut is sponsorship in politics? Listen to Trevor Phillips, a well-known TV producer in the United Kingdom, who spent many years in prominent roles in UK politics. He rose to be chair of London's Assembly and head of the United Kingdom's Equality and Human Rights Commission, but he got his political start while still a university student—thanks to a sponsor.

"In politics," Phillips says, "if you are part of this guy's gang, then everybody knows it. It's absolutely clear to everyone that part of your job is to support him and part of his job is to help you. It is a deal. Sponsorship is always a deal."

Phillips's start came in the 1970s, when he gave a speech at the convention of the United Kingdom's National Union of Students (NUS). Afterward, a young man named Charles Clarke came up to him. Phillips grew up in a North London community of working-class immigrants from the Caribbean, while Clarke came from the other, posh side of the tracks. But Clarke knew political talent when he saw it. "What do you want to do with your life?" he asked Phillips, who muttered something about finishing his chemistry degree and getting a job.

"Why don't we get you on the NUS executive committee," Clarke said, "and one day you could be its president."

In the United Kingdom, the National Union of Students is a big deal. It represents millions of students, owns real estate, and runs businesses—travel, catering, insurance—with thousands of employees and hundreds of millions in revenue. The NUS's executive positions are full-time jobs; holders typically take a sabbatical from university or serve just after graduation. The NUS presidency is in the national spotlight and is often a launching pad for a career in politics.

For this important opportunity, naturally Clarke didn't sponsor Phillips all at once. It took two years for him to fully commit. "I could have disappointed him," Phillips says. "I could have failed, and he would have dropped me like a stone, which he did with other people, and as I've done too with others in the years since."

Nor did Clarke act out of the goodness of his heart. He wanted to be president of the NUS himself, and he wanted his presidency to be a success. For that, he needed protégés who would round up votes for him at the election; once NUS president, he would need protégés on the executive committee to run the organization and its businesses competently, and to whip up votes for his policies at the student conventions. Last but not least, Clarke also understood the power of having a black man on his team. "At the time, there'd never been a non-white member of the NUS executive committee," Phillips says, "but a sixth of the NUS members were people of color. Charles said to me, 'We can't carry on like this.'"

With Clarke's help, two years later, Phillips was on the NUS executive committee, its first black member. And with the help of Phillips and Clarke's other protégés in the NUS, Clarke was indeed elected NUS president and made a success of it.

As part of the deal, Clarke continued to guide Phillips, who gave his sponsor not just stellar performance and a value add (his connection to the one-sixth of the NUS who were people of color), but loyalty too. "I learned an enormous amount from Charles," Phillips says. "And as a practical matter, some things I wouldn't always agree with him about, but there was never anything on which I refused to support him."

Two years after his election to the NUS executive committee, Phillips, "going in Charles's slipstream" as he puts it, became NUS president too. For Phillips as for Clarke, the NUS was the beginning of a political career. It was Clarke's introductions and counsel that enabled Phillips to eventually become a Labour Party politician.

Decades later, when the government created a new elected position—mayor of London—Phillips considered running for it. Once again, his old sponsor (by now a cabinet minister) was there for him with guidance and advocacy. "Charles advised me against it. He deemed it a 'celebrity position' with little real power. He wanted me in Parliament instead. But he still said, 'I'm going to support you if you want to do this.'"

Phillips ended up taking a different path, and with Clarke's support became chair of London's Assembly. He then left electoral politics, returning to a flourishing career as a TV producer and broadcaster, where he was still able to help his old sponsor.

"I was able to give Charles and his side of government more airtime and more of a fair hearing," Phillips says, "at a time when many television journalists were ardent supporters of his opponents."

So: Clarke helped Phillips, Phillips helped Clarke, Clarke helped Phillips again, and so it went, back and forth, over the years and decades. That's how sponsorship works. It's practical. It's based on respect. It requires both sides to make an effort. It provides reciprocal benefits. It's enduring. And it's usually part of a cascade: Phillips has had other sponsors over the years, and he's sponsored many others in turn.

That's the big picture of sponsorship, and Phillips, like most highly successful men and women, grasped its importance early on. For me, it was more of a journey, and I first truly understood its importance when I was looking for the answer to a different question.

Sponsorship Research

By the early 2000s, it was clear that women and people of color had a problem: in midlife their careers stalled, while white men with equivalent qualifications kept rising. The further up the management ranks you looked, the fewer women and people of color you found. It's a trend that has persisted to the present. In the United States today, middle management is 34 percent women and 27 percent people of color, but at the very top, it's almost all white men: only 4.2 percent of *Fortune* 500 CEOs are women and only 3.8 percent are people of color.[1,2,3]

I set out to find out why. An economist by training, I'm intrigued by numbers, and the numbers showed that many commonly given explanations didn't apply. Women and people of color were performing as well as white men. They had similar credentials. They were just as ambitious. Balancing motherhood and career was a challenge for some women, but nearly all women (nonmothers as well as mothers) at some point hit that glass ceiling, while men continued to advance.

I had a hunch: maybe women and people of color, lacking membership in the old boys' club, didn't have as many advocates in high places. I knew that plenty of women and other historically underrepresented groups had mentors, who were willing to give a little advice. But did they have sponsors, willing to go to bat for them, and with the clout necessary to make their advocacy matter?

I committed to digging deeper and in 2008 I plunged in, working with my research team at CTI to assemble hard evidence and pulling in executives from CTI's member companies for guidance. Many of these corporate leaders were eager to be helpful because they were interested in better understanding the dynamics for advancement within their own ranks.

The survey we conducted (introduced in chapter 1) found that my hunch was right: men were 46 percent more likely than women to have a sponsor.[4] Did this explain why so many women were falling behind their male peers? Kerrie Peraino, now leader of people operations for Google's global advisory functions, worked closely with me on this research. "Women and men were similar in most areas," she says. "The one change factor was the pivotal relationship they had or didn't have with someone of importance. That relationship accelerates progression." Looking further into the data, we found that this "sponsorship gap" also applies to ethnicity: Caucasians are 63 percent more likely than people of color to have a sponsor.[5] "Sponsorship isn't just a women's issue," Peraino says. "All talent needs it."

We continued our work by interviewing scores of managers, holding focus groups with hundreds more, and working closely with some of the world's biggest companies. The result of this work was a 2010 *Harvard Business Review* report, "The Sponsor Effect: Breaking Through the Last Glass Ceiling."[6] It showed, with hard data and concrete, on-the-record examples from corporate America, how sponsorship can empower those who have earned it to reach the very top. As Kerrie Peraino, who is a coauthor of this report (and an expert hand at sponsorship, as we'll see later), put it, "When sponsorship is done right, it's the great equalizer."

In the years since the publication of that report in 2010, my team and I, along with partners from a range of companies, have drilled down further into sponsorship: how it works, why it sometimes fails, and how best to tap its power. We've fielded several more surveys, conducted hundreds of interviews, and gotten hands-on experience helping roll out over thirty different sponsorship initiatives at major companies across the United States, including Credit Suisse, Intel, American Express, and Audible.

The sponsorship phenomenon is universal, we found. Woman or man, black or white, gay or straight, working in India, the United States, or Brazil, it's the same: if you have a sponsor, you're more likely to get ahead.[7]

But it's not just the protégé that finds benefits in this relationship. Over the last few years CTI and I have moved our attention to the other side of the equation: the benefits to the sponsor. The data shows that these benefits are tremendous.

How Sponsorship Boosts Sponsors

Sponsorship benefits sponsors at every stage of their career. Whether entry-level professionals, in the middle ranks, or senior executives, men who have a protégé are on average 20 percent more likely to report satisfaction with their rate of professional advancement. For women, the career boost from having a protégé is 13 percent.[8]

Those were the first big numbers on the sponsor dividend that we found, back in 2012. In the years since, as our surveys have multiplied, we've found more rigorous, data-driven evidence on how protégés boost their sponsors in every career level and across ethnicity, nationality, and gender. CTI's latest research, synthesized in figure 2-1, demonstrates these benefits in detail.

Senior-level managers, for example, are 53 percent more likely (46 percent versus 30 percent) to have received a promotion in the last two years, if they have a protégé. Entry-level professionals in our sample who have a protégé are 167 percent more likely (16 percent versus 6 percent) to have received a stretch assignment than those who don't.

Life has few certainties, but a 53 percent better chance of getting a promotion when you're already near the top, or a 167 percent

FIGURE 2-1 THE PAYOFF OF SPONSORSHIP

Responses to the following statements, by job level:

○ **Do not have a protégé**   ● **Have a protégé**

I have received a promotion in the past two years.

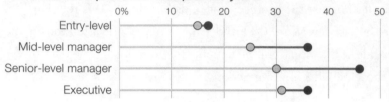

I have received a stretch assignment in the past two years.

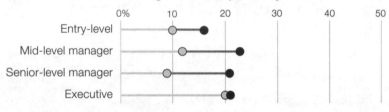

Source: Center for Talent Innovation

---

better chance of a stretch assignment when you're just starting out are impressive returns for taking on a protégé.

But perhaps the most startling fact about this data is that most of these sponsors are reaping impressive benefits *without* doing sponsorship right. When they do, the benefits grow still further. For example, male sponsors who have a protégé *and* have actively advocated (as only 30 percent did) for their protégé to receive a promotion are *twice as likely* as those without protégés to receive a promotion themselves.

The benefits extend far beyond short-term boosts, such as a one-time promotion. Among our survey respondents, who ranged from entry-level professionals to C-suite executives, 39 percent of those with a protégé deemed themselves "satisfied with their professional legacies" at this moment of their careers. Only 25 percent of those who don't have protégés said the same.

Yet the data also reveals a challenge. Across the board, we see that most self-identified "sponsors" aren't doing such a great job at it. They're leaving significant value on the table.

Three Sponsorship Gaps

If you're sponsoring someone, you presumably see some value in the relationship. But CTI's data indicates that many managers and executives who self-identify as sponsors fail to see how great that value could be—for themselves. They don't see that they're not doing their protégés a favor. They're developing their protégés, certainly, but skilled sponsors are also creating the conditions for their own greater success, and for their organizations to thrive. For you to succeed as you rise higher and higher, you'll need trusted, superbly competent lieutenants on your team; and for an enterprise to prosper, it needs its leaders to identify, include, inspire, instruct, and inspect its top talent.

But the data shows that many sponsors fall short in three main ways.

The Inclusion Gap

To get the most out of sponsorship, you need one or two protégés who are different from you. They can be a different gender or race; they can speak a different language or have a different skill set; they can have a different management style. The point is that a protégé can add the most value if they can provide something that you lack. But only 23 percent of sponsors look for a protégé who has attributes that they do not have. Over three-quarters of sponsors (77 percent) look for a "mini-me."

One fact that that helps explain this distressing reality is the exclusive nature of most social circles. In CTI's survey data, close to half of all white employers (41 percent) report that their immediate social network is missing either black, Hispanic, or Asian individuals.

Even those sponsors who attempt to connect with young high-performing talent across lines of difference often fail to do so effectively. For white sponsors, the most common description (51 percent) of how they attempt to connect with a protégé of a different ethnicity, is to "ask questions about their career path."

In some cases this approach can be effective, but without great care it can come across as a grilling or an interrogation, not as the beginning of a warm, supportive relationship. In the CTI survey, when asked what was most likely to inspire loyalty to their sponsor, many protégés did cite help in shaping their careers (50 percent), but a higher number yearned for a sponsor who was friendly (66 percent) and whom they liked personally (57 percent).

All of which makes sense. You may respect and be grateful to someone who offers you useful advice about your skill gaps or career goals. But deep loyalty to a person comes from realizing that this manager or leader believes in you, respects you, and is eager for an authentic exchange.

Sponsors of color are better at these kinds of bonding, our survey showed. The most common tactic (52 percent) they cite for connecting with protégés of a different race or ethnicity is "finding common interests" in activities that happen outside of work: travel, theater, or sports.

The Inspection Gap

The second common mistake we found is an especially dangerous one: a failure to thoroughly "inspect" a protégé for trustworthiness. Sponsors are likely to vet a prospective pick on performance: making sure that he or she works long hours and hits the numbers. But performance should really be table stakes. Surely your organization has many young top performers! What you should be concerned about when evaluating a potential protégé is loyalty to you and the organization. You don't want to use up precious political capital on a protégé who is secretly applying for a job with a competing firm, or, even worse, complaining about your management style to your boss.

In CTI's survey, the most common reason (73 percent) sponsors give as to why they've ended a relationship with a protégé is disloyalty. When a protégé bad-mouths you behind your back, or betrays you in some other way, he or she gets struck off the list.

The Investment Gap

A protégé can significantly increases a sponsor's scope and span over the long run. Think of how Sheryl Sandberg spoke up for Larry Summers ten years after he first took her on as a protégé; and how Maverick Carter, some twenty years after LeBron James first took an interest in him, helped James win a billion-dollar endorsement check. But despite the depth and duration of these payouts, CTI data shows that sponsors tend not to invest in their protégés for as long a time period as they should. Nor do they invest vigorously enough.

CTI data shows that 38 percent of sponsors at the senior management level or above say that in their experience, the sponsor-protégé relationship lasts two years or less. This is short-sighted. If you've found someone who can deliver top performance, impeccable loyalty, and a set of attributes you lack, why would you get rid of them? You should want them at your side for many years so that they can continue to deepen your capacity, expand your reach, and boost your brand. Neither Summers nor James would have gotten such enormous benefits if they'd shut the door after two years.

Another dramatic piece of data—which surprised me despite ten years of experience helping leaders perfect their sponsorship skills—is that only 30 percent of male sponsors and 24 percent of female sponsors advocate strenuously for a promotion for their protégés.

Certainly, some of these relationships are at early stages and sponsors may not be ready to fully commit. Yet these are low numbers. Clearly, many sponsors do not fully comprehend how deeply reciprocal sponsorship is. Rule of thumb: the more significant the investment, the bigger the payout. CTI data shows that protégés are more likely to come through on "mission-impossible" assignments when sponsors advocate for them vigorously.

Improving the Process

The good news here is that, if sponsors are already getting impressive benefits despite making serious mistakes, just imagine how much they—and their organizations—would gain if they started doing things right.

More and more leaders, do, after all, see sponsorship's power to boost protégés. But many lack insight into how the sponsor-protégé relationship can benefit them and the companies they work for. At a concrete level, they need to understand how sponsorship increases productivity, improves market access, burnishes their brand, and builds out legacy. And to realize all that value, they need to know, at a granular level, how to be a standout sponsor: how to identify, develop, and deploy a portfolio of protégés who can really deliver, who are worth the effort and the risk.

In part 2, I'll describe in detail the steps you need to take to build mutually beneficial and high-impact sponsorship relationships. But first, let's take a close look at what the payoffs look like "up close and personal" in the real world.

3

Payoffs for Sponsors

What is sponsorship worth to a sponsor? As the data in chapters 1 and 2 illustrated, it accelerates promotion and professional satisfaction, for a start. But it can do much more than that: it can open your organization to new markets; provide loyalty that you can rely on; get the scut work done so you can focus on where you add most value; position you to shine in top management's eyes; and help you reinvent a legacy enterprise for the new economy.

Open New Markets

$1.4 billion. That's the business that Todd Sears brought to Subha Barry some fifteen years ago, when he opened up a market to which she'd previously had no access.

In late 2001, Barry was a managing director at Merrill Lynch, in charge of multicultural business development for wealth management.

Her job was to help Merrill make a profitable business out of serving diverse communities.

Starting with her own South Asian community, then expanding to offer tailored services to African Americans, Hispanics, and women, Barry was already doing a great job at making diversity profitable for Merrill's global wealth management division.

Sears, a wealth adviser at Merrill, saw her success and came to her with an idea. He wanted to create a national campaign to market wealth management services tailored to the LGBTQ community, and he had a new model in mind for doing it. Instead of leveraging other organizations, as Barry had done through partnerships with professional groups such as the American Association of Physicians of Indian Origin, Sears would use his contacts in the LGBTQ community to market Merrill's services directly.

"Just as I had great familiarity with the South Asian community," Barry recalls, "he had a very personal experience in and knowledge of the LGBTQ community that would've taken us a lot of research and money to replicate."

Sears had previously proposed his idea to the broader marketing group within Merrill, but they had turned him down. They didn't see the LGBTQ community as a significant market. Barry did. But she didn't say yes to him—not yet.

"He had a couple of challenges," she says. "The first was that he was not a particularly successful wealth adviser. I had been very successful by the time I went to my senior leadership and asked them to support me. He was a rookie who had no credibility with senior leadership.

"So gave him fifteen thousand dollars and said, 'Use this to build a marketing effort around that community and show us what you can produce on your own. You have to first prove this with your own book of business. Then we can show the company that we've got a great opportunity for us to go national.'"

Sears delivered. "Within a year, year and a half, he brought in the assets," Barry says. "The multiplier was quite tremendous. I don't remember how much his business grew at the start, but I have to tell you, the order of magnitude was tremendous. He took that fifteen thousand we gave him and he showed us that if we invested in that community, there was enormous business to be done."

He also proved that his model, going direct to the community, would work.

"Whether through sponsoring an event, or holding a get-together for the LGBTQ community at a restaurant that they would usually go to, he used his background as a wealth adviser to create something that would allow him to position himself as a solutions provider," Barry recalls.

"Since you didn't have gay marriage at the time, he'd talk about things like, How do you title assets? What kind of legal documents should you sign? How do you allow your partner to have access, whether in the hospital or as next-of-kin in other circumstances? Here are some things you should pay attention to, so if something were to happen to you and your intent was to pass your assets on to your partner, it would be easy and simple.

"He approached it from the perspective of 'I'm educating you on what is possible. And of course if you do business with me at Merrill Lynch, you will have an adviser who already understands this and can help you with your money and broader planning.'"

She and Sears also grew a personal bond that helped her to trust him. "In many ways," Barry says, "as an Indian woman, I was an outsider at the company. So was he, as an 'out' financial adviser in a very conservative organization. So we were a pair of outsiders, and there was so much about him that reminded me of me, like his drive and desire to build something, to do something for his community. So I wanted him to be successful, and he never let me down. He never disappointed me. When he said he would do something, he delivered."

With Sears having proven himself, Barry's sponsorship ramped up. She got him a budget to go national, training financial advisers at Merrill offices around the country to serve the LGBTQ community. And she put him in touch with other parts of Merrill so that he could take advantage of the firm's sponsorship of cultural institutions popular among LGBTQ individuals.

"Whether it was the opera or museum—we sponsored Matisse and Picasso exhibits—we leveraged Merrill's support for iconic events in that area," Barry says. "It was really great because in learning how to do that we learned how to multiply the resources we had. It was actually with the LGBTQ community that we learned that we could engage the foundation, that we could engage other parts of Merrill to help fund our efforts. Then we did it with other communities too. It would be a Merrill sponsored event at a museum, and we would be allowed to invite the South Asian, the African American, the Hispanic, and the LGBTQ community, both financial advisers and their clients."

Sears created a national business that at its peak had over $1.4 billion in assets. So he was a success, but Barry had correctly assessed that she could trust him. Sears never forgot the sponsor who'd fought for him to have his big break and who had supported him every step of the way.

"There were a couple of very senior leaders at Merrill that were LGBTQ," Barry says. "Once he attained some prominence, he could very easily have gone around me to them, and he never, ever did. He was always generous about introducing me and others on my team to the LGBTQ community so we were set up for success."

Sears and Barry both left Merrill some years later, and Barry's successor lacked the vision to keep Sears's national program going. Instead he dispersed it to various branch offices and it lost. "Leadership didn't understand that you needed to keep a program like this going for five to seven years before it entered the DNA of the organization," Barry says sadly.

As a result, other companies seized this market. But the experience launched Sears and gave Barry a big success that continues to pay dividends. "I have so much credibility in the LGBTQ community," she says, "and it's because of Sears and how he started this work. He always shared the credit with me. Even today, he's still sharing the credit."

Leading with Yes

In September of 2016, Tiger Tyagarajan, CEO of the professional services giant Genpact, boarded a plane with a colleague, whom I'll call Saj.[1] Today Saj is a part of Genpact's senior management, but Tyagarajan first met him two decades ago, when Saj was a junior associate, twenty-three years old and fresh out of business school.

On this plane—a client's corporate jet—Tyagarajan and Saj were alone. "I sat down," Tyagarajan recalls, "and I turned to him and said, 'Time for your next job.' And he looked at me and said, 'What is it?' I told him: commercial leader for a certain business. 'Here's what that role entails,' I said. 'It'll involve a lot of deals, which you're good at. We need someone like you. It's a great move for you and I need you there. Next week.'

"The plane had just taken off and he said, 'Can I hop off right here, out the window?' We laughed, and he turned to me and said, 'Next week. Okay. I'm scared. I'm worried.' I thought he was going to say, 'I'm worried about this new job.' But he said, 'Where I am now, I own $7 million of bookings, the largest in the sales team. I'm worried what's going to happen. Who's going to take that job?'"

As Tyagarajan explains it, he had only moved Saj to his current position a few years before. Saj was leading an overhaul of sales and client relations for several of Genpact's most important business lines. Saj's job there, as he saw it, was far from done.

"I said, 'Of course. I need to find a replacement, but you don't need to do that. That's my job. You're moving.'

"He said, 'You're joking about next week, right? We'll do this in January. There are things that have to be done before I make the move.' He clearly thought I was just beginning a conversation about something that would ultimately happen. I said, 'No, I wasn't joking. Next week. Where you are now, they won't be easy shoes to fill, but I'll take care of that. You're moving. I need you there.'

"And he turned to me and said, 'Have I ever said no?'"

The reason why Saj never says no to Tyagarajan isn't that he's a pushover. On the contrary, he's a strong-minded, highly analytical, and fearless professional. But during his more than fifteen years of working under Tyagarajan, Saj has developed a trust in his leader and sponsor that more than justifies loyalty.

In the first years, as Tyagarajan recalls it, his sponsorship took the form of advice asked and given. "He reached out to me through the first few career moves and said, 'I've been told by someone in our organization of a job opportunity I've been invited to apply for. I want to talk to you, what do you think?' And each time I called him into my office, I'd listen to him, and I'd tell him, 'Yup, it's a good idea.' Or I'd tell him, 'Nope, don't do it. Here are the reasons. And if you need help from me to navigate that, tell me. If you don't need help, that's fine, but if you need help just say so.'"

Tyagarajan's advice was good. Saj kept finding himself growing and stretching, kept building new relationships, and—most important of all—kept delivering for Genpact.

As the years went by and Saj rose to become capable of performing roles that Tyagarajan had to fill directly, the senior man's guidance became firmer. "I would tap his shoulder and say, 'Saj, I have the next job for you.' Each time it's been about a five-minute conversation. And these are pretty significant shifts, from doing one thing to doing completely the opposite. He would say, 'Tiger, if you want me to do that and you think there's a great reason to do it, and I've understood the reason, then I'm in. What do you want me to do next?'"

About eight years ago, for example, Tyagarajan told Saj he wanted him to move to the other side of the world. "I said, 'How comfortable are you moving globally? Here's this assignment.' And Saj said, 'Let me just talk to my wife, and I'll come back to you tomorrow. I don't think there's an issue. I'd love it.' Next day, he came to me and said, 'We're moving.'"

That move, from Saj's home country to a much bigger market, gave him global experience with sales teams, important clients and prominence in the firm. "He's been amazingly successful," Tyagarajan says.

Even today, when Saj has significant power and a reputation inside and outside Genpact, this special relationship—Tyagarajan deciding where he and Genpact need Saj, and Saj immediately going and delivering—continues.

"Last week," Tyagarajan says, "as we were having a beer, he told me, 'When you moved me into this role, I didn't know why. It was so small and I had been doing this big job. I didn't know what I was going to do. But it's been this amazing fifteen months. The amount of learning I've had, I would never have expected it. Now I realize why you did what you did.'

"And then I looked at him and said, 'I think it's time to move you.' And he was having his beer, and he put his beer down and said, 'Where am I going now?'"

Trust, Loyalty—and Getting Work Done

Lydia Bottegoni today is senior vice president for story and franchise development at Blizzard Entertainment, maker of some of the world's most successful video games, including World of Warcraft and the Diablo series. She's also had a successful career as a Hollywood film producer.

But midway through that career in Hollywood, she made a decision that shocked her boss and many of her colleagues. Lydia at the time was moving her way up as a visual effects producer with Sony, where she'd been for about five years. "I was really on a pretty high note at that point," she recalls. "I had just finished a project that had ended really well and was very favorably received."

Then a woman named Carolyn Soper called her up. She told Lydia, "I am signing up to make an animated movie, and I really need your help. I'm trying to put together a team that I really know and trust. I would really love to have you work on this project with me. Is there any way you would leave Sony?"

The position would involve greater risk than Lydia's current one, it would be "a little bit of a demotion," as she recalls it, and it would take her out of the fast track she was on at Sony.

Lydia said yes.

"The boss I had at the time said, 'What do you mean, you're going to leave? You're on a high right now. You're doing great things and going places. We're on a great path with you. You're well regarded here, well respected. I'm really excited about the opportunity in front of you at this company. This is not the time to leave.' And I said, 'She's asked me to come help her, and I'm going to do it because this relationship is hugely important to me.'"

Lydia continued: "Sony counteroffered with a bunch of new money, a new title. I think they actually initially thought I was just doing this to leverage my position and get a raise and a new title out of it, but I actually wasn't. So they offered me a raise and a new title, which just made it actually made it an even harder thing for me to do to leave. But I did it anyway, and I did it 100 percent out of my loyalty to Carolyn and my belief that there was a lot to be gained by getting exposure to her and learning from her."

What did Carolyn do to inspire this kind of trust and loyalty? It began almost ten years earlier, when Lydia was a middle manager at a Citibank branch in an LA suburb, with no idea that her dream career in the entertainment business was possible.

"I had no formal training in filmmaking whatsoever," she says. "I had been an economics major." But she knew Carolyn, a visual effects producer at Disney. "We happen to be gay women, lesbians, so there was a little circle of us that were friends, and somebody was dating somebody else's friend. That was how we had all become socially connected."

They chatted about their work, as friends do, and Carolyn said to her one day, "You know what's interesting, you have more overlap with the job that I do than I think that you would ever believe. Because as much as I'm a creative person and I come from a creative background, I find that what I spend most of my time doing is juggling budgets and managing spreadsheets, and those are not really the muscles that I'm trained to use, and that part's a little uncomfortable for me."

As Lydia recalls, "I somewhat jokingly replied, 'Let me know when you're ready to hire me.'"

A few months later, the call came. "Carolyn said, 'I don't know if you really were serious at all, but I have an opportunity at Disney. We're looking for somebody. It's very entry-level, but if you want a foot in the door and are interested in this industry, this is really the only way for you to do it.'"

Lydia took it, leaving her career in finance. "I always joke," she says, "that coming out as a gay woman was an easier conversation with my parents than telling them I was leaving my management job in banking to take an entry-level job in filmmaking."

Carolyn had a rule at the time—she didn't work with friends. So she arranged to have Lydia placed on a different team in her division, where she reported to someone else. But the division was small—about thirty or forty people. That meant that job functions overlapped.

Carolyn taught Lydia what she couldn't pick up on the job, the technical terms and skills that her colleagues had learned in film school. And Lydia, excited and grateful to see a dream career possibly come true, did pretty much anything Carolyn needed.

"I had specific assignments with specific tasks," she says. "But we were a production entity, so new projects and new films would always be starting and ending. It was often the case that when one kicked off, the workload wasn't fully understood and we were not yet staffed up. So until we got the entire crew together, for those first couple of weeks, there were questions like, Who's going to do the film run?, or, Who's going to start renders?

"When Carolyn asked for volunteers to 'pitch in and take on extra work?' my response was immediate, I'd always raise my hand and say I'd do it," Lydia recalls.

The latest and least creative job of the day, for example, was usually hers.

"And at the end of the night," Lydia said, "somebody had to break down that film—these were the days of actual, physical film—and put it in a can in the darkroom. Then you had to drop it off at the lab, and oftentimes that didn't happen until the very end of the day, nine or ten at night. So it meant I stayed until late, and I not only broke down the film magazines and loaded up the film cans, I also drove them down to Hollywood and dropped them off at the lab."

These labs were a thirty-minute drive in the wrong direction from Lydia's home and in a seedy part of town.

That's how many sponsorship relationships start: with a senior person offering an opening, introductions, and instructions, and the junior person doing whatever it takes for her sponsor to succeed. When well done, this relationship creates lasting mutual benefits and loyalty.

When Carolyn left Disney, she handed off several projects to Lydia. And then Carolyn hired her old unit at Disney—and got Lydia assigned to do the work. "I still didn't really have the credentials to be a producer in my own right," Lydia says. "But she set me up to have an opportunity that I wouldn't have gotten for many years if not for her."

When, five years later, Carolyn needed her, Lydia was there for her. They still are there for each other today, a time when both women are big successes in their field.

"It's a relationship that's been twenty-five years in the making," Lydia says. "We're dear friends, and she's still the person I reach out to when I'm making a hard decision."

Shine in Leadership's Eyes

When Melinda Wolfe took the top job in human resources at Bloomberg in 2008, the company wasn't just famous for having redefined financial data and journalism. It was also infamous for its hard-driving, unforgiving, and sometimes abusive culture.

"We simply throw everyone interested into the deep end of the pool, as it were, and stand back," Michael Bloomberg wrote in a 1997 memoir. "It becomes obvious very quickly who the best swimmers are." That macho culture led to a high burnout rate—and legal problems. The magazine *Portfolio* published a profile of the firm just a few months after Melinda Wolfe arrived. It listed multiple lawsuits over sexual harassment and gender bias, as well as expensive payouts to settle them. One lawsuit was a class action alleging discrimination against pregnant women and mothers. Women also reported leaving the company not because they disliked the work, but because they disliked the culture.[2]

Such was the situation that Wolfe had to fix. Some changes—such as introducing flextime and the possibility of work-at-home schedules for parents—management could introduce with the stroke of the pen. Others, such as making sure mothers and other caregivers felt confident that they could actually request that flextime, without suffering negative repercussions, were trickier.

Wolfe had to change not just the rules but the culture. Throwing everyone in the deep end to see who sinks and who swims might work with a small company. It doesn't work with a multinational media and technology juggernaut that has to recruit, cultivate, incentivize, and retain tens of thousands of employees, of both genders and all backgrounds, all over the world.

And here was the even trickier part: large elements of that macho culture thought that everything was fine, just as it was; that human resources in general and Wolfe's role in particular were, at best, window dressing to help quell legal problems, and at worst, a waste of everyone's time. So she not only had to do her job; she also had to convince people that her job was worth doing. HR, as big companies understand it, hardly existed at Bloomberg when Wolfe came on board.

Wolfe couldn't accomplish this transformation on her own—so she reached out to a younger woman whom she knew professionally but had never worked with directly before. Like Wolfe, Anne Erni was an HR professional who had started off in financial services, in her case, on the trading floor. They'd both later worked in diversity and inclusion (Wolfe at American Express, Erni at Lehman Brothers) and they'd met many times.

Wolfe knew that Erni had the soft skills—relationship building and tact—that she wanted at her side. She knew too that Erni had what Bloomberg needed: a different, "less Darwinian" way of thinking about HR. Finally, she knew from Erni's background on Wall Street that she knew how to maneuver inside a hard-driving, even cutthroat workplace.

She knew, in short, that Erni was a high performer. What she didn't know was whether Erni would be able to do the nitty-gritty of building an HR function from the ground up. She'd never done that kind of heavy lifting before.

"I needed someone who wasn't only building relationships, but would put rigor, process, and thought behind, for example, building out succession benches and identifying top talent," Wolfe says. "And we needed someone who could start from scratch, because none of those functions even existed at Bloomberg, which also lacked a robust learning and development function."

Wolfe thought that Erni was the right person, but she couldn't be sure. So she didn't hire her outright. She brought her in as a contractor for a series of specific tasks. Erni excelled at these tasks and soon took on new ones.

"She threw herself into subject matter that she really didn't know," Wolfe says. "She learned it quickly and created solutions that had business impact." Erni also helped restructure and recreate Bloomberg's learning function, so that the company no longer just threw people into the deep end, but instead identified high-potential employees and taught them how to swim.

Where Erni particularly added value to Wolfe was in the most important and delicate part of Wolfe's mission: nudging a culture toward change, when many longtime leaders at the company didn't want it to change one bit.

"Erni quickly figured out the culture wasn't going to accept cookie-cutter solutions or any of the standard toolkits for HR. People at Bloomberg didn't like to do anything that looked like what everybody else did. So she innovated around that and not only came up with new procedures, but also created and led processes so that people would actually use the new procedures," says Wolfe.

For example, rather than using the HR standard "nine box" to judge potential and talent, Erni came up with a sophisticated alternative, involving customized heat maps, to both get the job done and get long-term employees excited about using it.

Delighted, Wolfe began both to shift more responsibility to Erni and to give her more coaching. She needed to help Erni learn how to talk to the technologists who dominated Bloomberg, a far cry from the bankers Erni had worked with before. As Wolfe made more and more introductions for Erni, advocating for her with senior management, she truly became her sponsor. "I was increasingly investing in her. Her success was my success."

Then when a staff position opened up—head of leadership, training, and diversity—the opinion of senior management was unanimous: "They said, 'Anne Erni is the right choice, and we're willing to do what it takes to bring her in formally.'"

Over the next few years, Wolfe and Erni worked side by side to make Bloomberg's culture welcoming for a wide range of talent, and to ready its HR team to identify and advance a diverse pool of top talent into Bloomberg's leadership ranks.

"I needed someone like Anne, because I couldn't change the whole company on my own," Wolfe says, "And besides, the sheer quality of her work upped my game, made me look good, and allowed senior leaders to grasp how important my role was. They now understood that HR could add enormously to the value of the company by finding and cultivating talent. She really made a difference in helping the company value my work."

When Wolfe left Bloomberg, it was only natural that she'd recommend that Erni replace her and that Erni would get the job. Erni thus helped Wolfe not just succeed in her position, but enabled her to leave a legacy behind—a subject I'll address in this book's last chapter.

Reinvent the Organization

"Disruption" may have become a buzzword, but if you're in advertising, it's a day-to-day reality. As consumers have gone digital and mobile, and as traditional clients increasingly want alternatives to keeping a firm on a long-term retainer, the "Big Four" agencies have had to reinvent themselves.

"In this business today, if you want to grow, you've got to be comfortable with being uncomfortable," Lou Aversano, CEO of Ogilvy & Mather in New York (a division of WPP), told me. "You have to be willing to burn your lifeboats before someone burns them for you." Yet industry veterans such as himself face a challenge that he calls "altitude."

"We see things from a certain height, and we have biases based on our years of experience and established ways of getting things done," he explains. So when Aversano took the helm in 2014 and started a strategic transformation, he reached out to millennial talent that didn't look at things from this same altitude.

For that, Aversano tapped one of Ogilvy's employee resource groups, the Young Professionals Network. He tasked its one hundred members (average age twenty-seven) to offer ideas about how to reinvent the business model that underpinned the agency. But the process wasn't a suggestion box. Aversano and other senior leaders worked with these young executives closely for nearly two months, instructing them on the business challenges and offering feedback so they could grow their strategic chops and offer evolved, informed ideas.

One result of this initiative was a set of actionable insights for the agency, including a new staffing model that offers greater flexibility—benefiting the firm, whose staffing needs vary month-to-month—but still gives employees a sense of stability and loyalty. Another result was that Aversano identified a standout potential protégé: a young man named Ben Levine.

After working closely with Levine through the Young Professionals Network, Aversano was so impressed he put him on Ogilvy's leadership team as a "senior adviser for transformation." There, Levine has delivered transformative advice. For example, given his refreshing lack of altitude, Levine has been able to map out novel ways Ogilvy can engage with clients. He has also identified patterns that show which of the approaches are most likely to produce revenue and profit. "He's charted the path to growth for us," Aversano says.

Levine has also proven to be "a universal translator," as Aversano puts it, between other millennials and the leadership team. "We've had a very formal way of planning," Aversano says. "Ben and his peers are informal. There's less hierarchy, less fear, more brainstorming. Their mantra isn't *be perfect, criticize and challenge*, but instead *experiment and iterate*. Ben is able to distill this millennial sensibility, package it, and convert it into a voice that leadership can process and understand. So there's been a liberation in how ideas flow."

Those are big payoffs for this premier advertising firm and its CEO: a new staffing structure, a new path to growth, and a conduit to a younger generation's ways of thinking and working. So this relationship is providing valuable support to Aversano as he transforms Ogilvy for the coming decades.

Aversano and Levine, like the other pairs of sponsors and protégés in this chapter, are naturals at these reciprocal, enduring alliances. Yet it doesn't have to be all about instinct and intuition. There is a formula to getting it right.

In this book's next part, I'll present that formula in the form of a playbook, along with detailed examples from the business world and hard data to back it all up.

Part Two

---•---

THE PLAYBOOK FOR SUCCESS

4

Identify Potential
Protégés

How do you identify the right protégés to sponsor? You certainly have to spot top performers with a strong work ethic, but that's not enough. You want a protégé who will reward your investment by enabling you to work better; who will provide loyalty to both you and the organization; and who will fill a gap in your abilities and the enterprise's.

After all, you're not sponsoring someone just for your own benefit. You're also doing it for the sake of the enterprise where you work. If you're at the top of your organization (or planning to get there one day), you might even be sponsoring someone who will one day take the reins and perpetuate your vision.

In CTI's survey, we asked what sponsors look for in their protégés. The most common quality that they cited was indeed performance: 73 percent of our respondents called it out. Next came loyalty, which 62 percent of respondents said that they look for in a protégé. That's all logical: a highly able protégé who is committed to you and your agenda in the enterprise is a powerful support for a leader or for someone who intends to lead someday.

Interestingly, when we broke the data down by career stage, we found that middle managers are far more likely (80 percent) to cite the need for high performance in a protégé than senior managers or above (60 percent). That's because for those in mid-career, trying to prove their worth to clients and superiors, a top performer who can make them more productive is particularly highly valued. Of course those at or near the top already value ability too, but since they can summon top performers from across (or outside) the enterprise to assist them, it's not quite as critical. Such leaders, as we'll see, often see performance as table stakes.

To better understand how leaders choose protégés who will give them that career-enhancing payoff, let's look at how three highly successful people went about it. One is a legend in the insurance business who found the number two he needed when he started a new firm. The second is a prominent legal scholar whose protégé has enabled him to have a broader influence without sacrificing excellence as a revered professor and authority in his field. The third is the CEO of a multibillion-dollar multinational. His protégé delivers steller results and commitment.

For all three, choosing the right protégé was a big step in taking their careers and their influence to the next level.

Choosing a Right-Hand Person

Andrew Marks has had an impressive career in insurance: working his way up through industry giants, then starting his own firm, MLW (now a part of Arthur J. Gallagher), in 1986.

He started MLW with two partners, but he knew that they, like him, were primarily engaged in business development. He needed someone who would be there just for him, helping out in ways such as taking some of the technical and day-to-day client management work off his hands, so Marks would be free to "make rain" and build a client base for the new firm.

He chose, as sponsors often do, a man he had already worked with for years at his old job: Bruce Tindal. "Bruce was charming," Marks says, "he was honest, he was bright, and he broke his back for clients."

That last characteristic in particular caught his attention. "Bruce understood, you've got to kill yourself for clients. I don't care if it's midnight, if you get a request from a client, you've got to do it, you've got to have urgency, and he had it."

Marks describes how Tindal showed this urgency: "When I got a new lead, before we headed off for that first meeting, he'd do all the research, pull all the information together without me needing to ask him. And then he'd come back and show it to me. We'd discuss where to go from there, what a winning set of tactics would be. He'd pump me for what materials he needed to pull together for next steps given our emerging strategy. He would handle all of this accurately and urgently. Going out and doing research is one thing. Putting it all together into a winning offer is another."

For these reasons, when Marks started his own venture in the 1980s, he took a bet on Tindal. Marks recalls: "I went to him and told him straight, 'I'm going to set up on my own, and I want you to come. I can't offer you much except promises. It's going to be a brand-new firm, and I've never had my own firm. But I want you to come, because you're capable of great work, and I can teach you a ton of stuff about how to succeed in this business.' So he came. He knew that he had a lot to learn. He knew that he needed me as much as I needed him."

In the new firm, Marks introduced Tindal—an Irish American and the son of an auto mechanic—to his contacts in elite social circles of New York. He also taught him the nuts and bolts of their business.

"How to create programs, property and casualty programs," Marks explains. "We didn't sell off the shelf. Bruce had to learn how to customize offerings to meet the specific needs of individual clients. So I taught him."

With a trusted, skilled right-hand man, Marks could now go out and do what he does best: create new markets in places where few others would even think to look. "I figured out that in New York, a big part of the economy is not-for-profits and social service agencies," he says. "They need insurance too. And I know Jewish geography. They tease me in the business that I know more influential people in New York than maybe, perhaps, Michael Bloomberg."

From his perches at the Yale Club and Harmonie Club in Manhattan, Marks cultivated the leaders of the top Jewish philanthropies, worked with Tindal to create tailored products that these agencies needed, and went on to win the business. In the process, of course, he introduced his protégé, whose trustworthiness, charm, and unrelenting urgency made him a hit.

"He's so well liked, if I get hit by a bus tomorrow, he'd hold onto the accounts I brought in," Marks says.

Finding a Lieutenant to Expand Your Influence

In 2016, Kenji Yoshino already had what some might consider three full-time jobs. As Chief Justice Earl Warren Professor of Constitutional Law at New York University's School of Law, Yoshino is one of the country's most influential legal scholars. It's his job to produce original research that shifts public discourse, and that's what he does with great distinction. He publishes regularly in the *Harvard Law Review*, the *Stanford Law Review*, the *Yale Law Journal*, and other legal journals. He also reaches a wider public through articles in the *Los Angeles Times*, the *New York Times*, and the *Washington Post*.

Yoshino also has to give NYU law students the high-quality teaching that they demand. Here too, he delivers. He won NYU Law's Podell Distinguished Teaching Award in 2014.

Finally, Yoshino is an author who's published three widely acclaimed books: *Covering: The Hidden Assault on Our Civil Rights*; *A Thousand Times More Fair: What Shakespeare's Plays Teach Us About Justice*; and *Speak Now: Marriage Equality on Trial*.

Besides work, Yoshino and his husband are raising two children, and he's helping steer his alma mater: he was elected to the Harvard Board of Overseers in 2011 for a six-year term, and he served as its president in the 2016–2017 academic year.

Yoshino doesn't sound like a man who had time to take on a big new responsibility. But that's exactly what he did in 2016 when he founded the Center for Diversity, Inclusion, and Belonging at NYU Law School. The center fosters interdisciplinary research and course offerings on diversity and inclusion at NYU, brings in speakers (including several supreme court justices), and provides the law school and a number of outside institutions with thought leadership and executive education.

How does Yoshino manage it all? With the help of a protégé.

In an interview, Yoshino told me that he got the idea of a protégé from the private sector. "I looked at many of my colleagues who are practicing law in a corporate environment," he says. "Those who were really leveraging their talents and having an impact on issues they cared about were those who could get others to help them execute their ideas."

Yoshino spotted a potential protégé quite quickly: an exceptionally well-qualified newly minted young lawyer. But it took several years for the relationship to deepen.

David Glasgow first came to Yoshino's attention as one of his students. In Yoshino's words, "He was a star performer, head and shoulders above most of the students I've encountered in my career." Yoshino wasn't alone in thinking that: Glasgow would graduate number one in his year, with the top GPA in the program. But Glasgow was more than a good student. In class he demonstrated presence, tact, and the ability "not just to command a room, but to read a room," Yoshino says.

So Yoshino hired him as a research assistant for his book *Speak Now: Marriage Equality on Trial* and soon saw that Glasgow was more than just a brilliant researcher. He had the proactive can-do energy and the loyalty and sensitivity to execute on Yoshino's behalf.

"He did everything from citation checking to copyediting to finding sources I had overlooked," Yoshino says. "He was ferocious in advancing my work and my work's quality. His interchanges with people, whether editors, assistant editors, or copyeditors, were spot on. Even when he was pushing back strongly on something for me, insisting that it be done our way, he was tonally right and respectful."

Once again, Yoshino received outside affirmation of his own positive impressions. "My editor told me that if Glasgow ever wanted a job in publishing, he'd hire him in a second. The work he did on my book was extraordinary."

When Yoshino decided to launch his new center in 2016, he realized that he needed more than just a research assistant. He needed someone who could take much of the burden off his shoulders and give him—Kenji Yoshino—that rarest of resources: more time in his life for his central responsibilities. So he offered Glasgow the job of executive director at the new Center for Diversity, Inclusion, and Belonging.

There, as Yoshino's protégé, Glasgow has cleared the high bar he set first as a student, then as a research assistant. All Yoshino has to do is set the goals and the guidelines, and Glasgow executes. "He frees me from the need to micromanage or even to manage the micromanager," Yoshino says.

For example, when Yoshino invited Supreme Court justice Sonia Sotomayor to speak at the center, he simply asked Glasgow to prepare for her visit. The rest—speaking arrangements, formal events at the law school, a party, logistics—Glasgow took care of.

For the other work of the center—including its flagship course for NYU law students on leadership, diversity and inclusion, and its executive education program—it's the same story: Yoshino provides the big ideas, often after discussion with Glasgow, then Glasgow executes. He's helped create curricula, administered surveys, performed statistical analyses, and made presentations.

But good protégés do more than free you from the little things so that you can work on the big things. They extend the scope and span of what you can do.

Yoshino has long considered a new version of his now classic book *Covering*, but he has hesitated. It isn't just that he doesn't have the time. It is that even though he sees a way to turn the book from a mix of law and memoir into a guidebook for organizations, a lot of the work and research that this new book would require simply doesn't interest him.

So Yoshino has decided to take another step in his sponsorship relationship and entrust Glasgow with a deeper responsibility: conducting and synthesizing research so that the forthcoming book—provisionally titled *Uncovering Talent*—will be even better than Yoshino could do on his own. Once again, Glasgow is delivering. "He's taking the parts that I find tedious and could be weaknesses, and really executing on them and making them strengths," Yoshino says. Little-by-little over the years Yoshino has entrusted Glasgow with more and more responsibility. At every incremental step, he's seen Glasgow deliver excellence and then trusted him with still more.

Lest it sound like Yoshino is exploiting Glasgow, let me make clear that Yoshino is more than fulfilling his part of the sponsor-protégé bargain. Besides experience, Glasgow is gaining a powerful résumé and network. He's executive director of a center at one of the country's most prestigious law schools, where he's meeting eminent legal scholars and other thought leaders. Thanks to Yoshino, Glasgow is now co-teaching a class at NYU—yet another star on his résumé. When *Uncovering Talent* is published, Glasgow will have coauthor credit. And when Glasgow became a father in 2017, Yoshino decided on his own (the contract didn't require it) to give him a generous paid parental leave.

It's a rewarding relationship for both of them, as the sponsor-protégé relationship has to be, because that relationship has to be deeply reciprocal and centered on trust—a subject our next sponsor has a lot to say about.

Choosing a Protégé Who Deserves Trust

Horacio Rozanski has been CEO of Booz Allen Hamilton (BAH), the consulting and technology giant, since 2015. When I asked him how he chose a protégé, he said that performance was a given. "At Booz Allen Hamilton, everyone in the upper ranks is smart and high-performing. That's not enough to set someone apart." What matters to him are things far more significant: commitment, integrity, and courage. "I can work through anything else," he says, "and I can teach anything else, but a person's values have to be aligned with mine and the organization's."

"When you sponsor a person, as the CEO, that person carries some of your authority," he explains. "The wrong person can abuse that authority. So, for a CEO sponsor, the most important thing about protégés is what they'll do when you're not watching."

How is it possible to find someone you can trust with that kind of authority? For Rozanski, the answer begins (but doesn't end) with working with the person directly over a period of time.

Consider one of his current protégés. In the early 2000s, when Rozanski was head of human resources at Booz Allen, the firm asked

him to reorganize its relationship with some of its most senior consultants and contractors. To assist him, senior management assigned him
a contracts specialist, Jen Wagner.

As part of her job, Wagner needed to represent Rozanski in
conversations with very senior executives. She had to persuade them
to accept a new way of working and a new structure for their compensation. Without fail, when she talked to them, they fell in line. "She
was dealing with some of the firm's most important people, people
very senior to her. She was very persuasive but she never gave an
inch," Rozanski told me. "And at the end of the day, they all liked her."

That was a huge value add for Rozanski, who was able to leave this
delicate task in her hands. "These guys, they were the firm's lions,
accustomed to having everything their own way," he says. "She got
those lions back on their stools, and most impressive of all, they were
happy about it."

After several months working with Wagner, Rozanski began to get
to know her personally too. He learned that she had another job, one
that many people would consider full-time: she was raising two children on her own.

"I think that's where her extraordinary combination of strength and
sympathy comes from," Rozanski told me. "If you're raising two kids on
your own, you don't have the luxury of giving part of the job to someone
else. You have to be good cop and bad cop at one and the same time."

Despite his appreciation of Wagner, it was another six years before
Rozanski arranged for her to work directly for him. By then, he was
Booz Allen's chief operating officer, and he needed a director of
operations. The person who filled this role would be his top assistant,
and would either enable or cripple his effectiveness. He thought of
Wagner, but he didn't rush forward. He asked others' opinions first.

"You need more than a hunch and one great experience to choose
a protégé," he says. "Before you throw your weight behind somebody,

you have to do your homework." For Rozanski, that homework involved not just talking to Wagner's bosses, but also to her coworkers and direct reports. After all, plenty of people are better at managing up than managing down. But that kind of person wouldn't have the values that Rozanski was seeking.

All that Rozanski heard from his sources convinced him that his initial impression was correct. He offered her the role of director of operations.

That was six years ago. Since that time, Rozanski has risen to CEO, and he's kept Wagner at his side. She's continued to show the judgment, ability, grit, and tact that first impressed him. She also gives him a gift that he can't give himself: honest feedback. "One of the reasons I love working with her is that she will on occasion come in my office, close the door, and let me have it. Nine out of ten times, I deserve it."

That's especially valuable, he says, because when you're at the top of an organization, it's hard to get real feedback. "You therefore need to pick people who have the courage to go into your office and tell you some uncomfortable facts. A protégé is the right person to do that. If you pick the right protégés, you're going to learn a lot."

That idea, learning from your protégés, is a big one. That's why Rozanski, like Yoshino, found a protégé who could deliver performance, loyalty—and something else. That something else is *difference*. Because one of the most powerful ways a protégé can enhance your career is if they bring to the table something that you don't have. Wagner came to Rozanski with the experience of single motherhood, which gave a different dimension to her leadership skills. Glasgow brought Yoshino a different, more granular, mind; one who could add to Yoshino's research a level of practical detail he could not provide himself.

Rozanski and Yoshino were both highly aware of the value of difference in their protégés, but this awareness isn't common. In CTI's survey, only 23 percent of sponsors said that they look for protégés who have skills or a management style that they lack.

But when you explicitly set out to look for that difference in a protégé, the value add can be enormous, as examples in our next chapter will show.

Breaking It Down

The journey to sponsorship begins with identifying the right people. Seeking out top performers is a given, but you must also consider trustworthiness and what gaps you may need to fill in terms of your own skill sets and capabilities, or those of your team. The tips below provide additional advice for how to find the best prospects and the best balance.

- **Start early.** A middle-level manager can benefit as much as a senior executive from being a sponsor. As we'll see in chapter 11, an ambitious young manager can leverage a high-performing protégé all the way to the top. Managers need to "shed the scut work" and expand their scope and span as much as executives.

- **Make demands.** Have high expectations and expect a protégé to deliver value from the outset. This is sponsorship not mentorship and reciprocity needs to be baked in from the start. The pace can vary. Yoshino was unusually deliberate and slowly ratcheted up the level of responsibility he placed on Glasgow's shoulders; Marks was much more urgent in his demands—indeed, an appreciation of the "urgency" of client needs was one of the traits he admired in his protégé.

- **Delegate the small stuff.** If you are on the fast track (and all sponsors are) time is your scarcest asset and you need to guard it jealously so that you have enough bandwidth for high-priority tasks. You therefore need the shed the tedious work in your life. Who better to take responsibility for a load of detailed, annoying stuff than a protégé who has skin in the game and is rooting for your success! Such a person is motivated and likely to take care of this work flawlessly.

- **Seek out loyalty and trustworthiness.** The data tells us that a protégé pick needs to clear a high bar on two fronts: performance and loyalty. As Rozanski points out, in the executives ranks stellar performance can be taken for granted and it behooves a sponsor to focus his or her attention on trustworthiness. This is particularly good advice given that when sponsorship breaks down, the break is more often caused by an erosion of trust rather than a shortfall in performance (see chapter 8).

- **Assess your gaps and needs—but don't limit yourself.** It's great to find a protégé who can complement your skills with a value add of their own. A tech-savvy millennial might bring to the table social media marketing expertise you don't have. But give some thought to what will support you not just now, but a few years down the line when you take your career to the next level. Don't let your immediate needs stop you from seizing an outstanding talent even if his or her competencies are not an obvious fit.

- **Look internally for some of your prospects.** Taking on a protégé is extraordinarily powerful—sponsorship boosts the promotion prospects of the younger person by close to 20 percent. Some executives and managers look to the outside (Tyagarajan is a case in point), but most organizations like leaders at every level to groom and grow internal talent—it's good for succession planning and for team morale. So bear organizational needs in mind as you construct your protégé portfolio.

5

Include Diverse Perspectives

When the late and much-missed Ed Gilligan was president of American Express, he made clear to senior executives that they should 1) pick three up-and-comers to sponsor and 2) make sure that *two* of these protégés didn't look like them. It became known as "Gilligan's one-plus-two rule."

What lay behind Gilligan's rule was a savvy insight. Gilligan was saying, sure, sponsor one high-performing younger talent who reminds you of yourself—a "mini-me," so to speak. But with the other two picks, mix it up. Reach across the divides of gender, generation, and culture to find high performers who bring to the table knowledge, skill sets, life experiences, and contacts that you lack—and that you and your organization need. Gilligan understood that when leaders build a diverse portfolio of protégés, sponsorship's power multiplies.

In other words, as I discussed in chapter 2, the best protégés are those who are high performers, can deliver loyalty, and provide a value add—and that value add will often be *difference*.

Unfortunately, looking for difference in a protégé isn't as common as it should be. CTI data shows that only 23 percent of sponsors look for a protégé who has attributes that they personally lack. Among boomers, who are most likely to be at the very top of organizations, the number is only 14 percent.

This insufficient attention to the value of difference extends to race: 53 percent of whites, 49 percent of blacks, and 40 percent of Hispanics are sponsoring, as their primary protégé, someone of their own race or ethnicity. This preference of sponsors for their own kind is simply a reflection of our segregated society. CTI survey data shows that fully 41 percent of white employees do not have an immediate social network that includes black, Hispanic, and Asian individuals.

Sponsorship is a powerful tool to break down barriers and expand networks and capabilities, both for the individual leader and for the enterprise. When you explicitly set out to include protégés who come from a different background, have a different identity, or bring a different skill set to the table, the benefits can be tremendous. Talent pools and growth markets are increasingly diverse and an inclusive portfolio of protégés can turbocharge a leader's journey.

Include Transformative Skills and Sensitivity

When Kevin Lord took the helm of the Fox News HR department at the start of 2017, he had his work cut out for him: the network faced high-profile allegations of sexual harassment and a class-action lawsuit alleging racial discrimination.[1] The atmosphere in parts of the organization was tense, to say the least.

To change the workplace environment in the minds of both current and prospective employees, Lord wanted to rebuild the HR department and transform the people culture at Fox News. In particular, he wanted to create a workplace where women and people of color would feel welcome, safe, and eager to contribute.

Lord, a fifty-something white man, needed allies to fulfill that goal. "I knew from a cultural standpoint," he says, "that I needed colleagues who could help me bridge the gap. I needed to bring in some people who looked different than me, who brought a different perspective, and who also signaled that at Fox News there are now different types of HR people."

Given Fox News' brand at the time, attracting talented women or people of color to the team wasn't going to be easy. But Lord knew at least one great prospect: Marsheila Hayes, a social media–savvy young black woman, a top performer in HR at another media giant, Gannett.

He called her—and got, at first, a definite maybe.

"When he called me up and said, 'I may have an opportunity at Fox,'" Hayes recalls, "my response was, 'Um, I don't know. I don't know about Fox.'"

"But," she says, "I took the job, because I trusted him as a leader. I still do."

How did this bond of trust, crossing generation, gender, and race, come to be? It began in 2012, when Lord too was at Gannett, as its head of HR.

"At Gannett," Lord says, "we had this talent development program, and we had guest presenters, and one day Marsheila, who was very junior, just a few years out of college, was asked to introduce the company's CEO. She did a fabulous introduction, funny, humorous, graceful. She just corralled the room, commanded and controlled it, while talking about the CEO in the CEO's presence! I said, *I want to know her.*"

At about the same time, Lord instituted a "reverse mentorship" program, in which a senior person partnered with a junior one who would teach the senior person digital skills—a big gap in Lord's own skill set. He chose Hayes to be his "reverse mentor," and, as he'd hoped, she offered him a great deal of insight into social networks and digital platforms, and her insights were actionable. For example, she helped Lord find a tech company to partner with, so Gannett could build virtual recruiting programs at universities.

Hayes also led Gannett's first virtual career fairs, which boosted recruitment not just among college graduates, but also among military veterans and people of color. She also increased the social media following of Gannett careers across Twitter and Facebook by 87 percent and 94 percent and chaired the company's first employee resource group for women.

Just as Hayes delivered for Lord, he delivered for her. As she recalls, "Kevin asked me, 'Within HR are there any areas that you haven't had experience in yet that you'd like to get exposure to? If so I can set up some shadowing opportunities for you.' In addition, when there were new and exciting projects going on, he would be very open to just adding me to the project team as an observer or as someone who could offer some insights from my place in the business. And that helped significantly to keep me on my toes and thinking strategically, not just about my little area of HR, but about the function in general."

Once they become comfortable with each other professionally, it was natural for the relationship to evolve into a collegial friendship. This closer connection very much centered on his kids and her career.

"Whenever I talked with Kevin about having a virtual career fair or a Skype session with one of the colleges," Haynes says, "I would ask, 'Would your son Zack like to attend something like that, where he'd learn about the Whitman School at Syracuse through a one-on-one Skype session?' And Kevin would appreciate the invitation and convey it to Zack. Or I would ask his opinion about a webinar and tell him that one of its advantages was that it would allow us to record and send it out to students who weren't able to be there in person. And he'd come right back to me with 'I like that. Then they could share it with me as a parent, and I could see it too.'"

His interest was authentic. Lord's children really were looking at colleges and careers, and given the fact Haynes was twenty years younger than Lord, it made sense that he would seek her advice on what his children could access and what they should be looking for. A little later on in their friendship, he asked her whether she knew recent alumni in his children's chosen fields whom they could talk to—which she did and happily made the connections.

Since Lord trusted Hayes enough to ask her advice, she returned the favor and asked his thoughts on her big life debate at the time: Should she go to graduate school? Was it a good experience? If so, which one? What had he gotten out of his graduate school experience? Did he know anyone she could talk to? He responded with the same thoughtfulness that she had given him and his children.

"That was something that I really appreciated about him," she says. "It wasn't just a matter of, 'Oh, yeah, go to grad school. Everyone should have a master's degree.' He really looked at it as: 'If you want to be successful, this would be a great opportunity for you because of A, B, and C, but this is the due diligence that you need to do, and don't just look at the academics. Really examine the worth of the professional network this degree feeds into and how the school would help you access it. Also take a hard look at how this degree would add value to your career going forward.'"

Hayes ended up deciding to get her master's at Georgetown, which she did in the evenings, while still performing at her customary, exceptional level at Gannett. It was a great experience.

This growing personal trust between Lord and Hayes deepened the trust that they already shared at work. When Gannett changed health benefits in a way that led to some employee discontent, Lord felt comfortable enough with Hayes to lean on her—it was Hayes whom Lord counted on, even though he was the head of HR and she was very junior—to give him insights into how employees were really feeling.

"It was like truth serum," he says. "You get to a senior level in an organization and people don't want to tell you the truth. They want to tell you what they think you want to hear. Marsheila didn't do that. She told me what I *needed* to hear. Not naming names but telling me how people in general were talking about the changes."

When Gannett split into two businesses, Lord and Hayes ended up in different companies. But they continued to stay in touch, and when two years after that Lord left to become head of HR at Fox News, the two had an established level of trust that enabled Lord to reach out to Hayes—and that enabled Hayes to say yes.

At Fox, Hayes's title is director of campus programs and diversity outreach, but that only hints at her value to Lord. She's his point person for working with the plaintiffs in many of the lawsuits that the network is facing. He's also tasked her with leading investigations into several accusations, and to support that, he assigned her to work with the CFO on the design of updated policies in this area.

All that visibility has been a big plus for Hayes but it has also helped Lord put out fires. The fact that she is a high-profile black woman is important. As he puts it, "There are a lot of diverse people who feel comfortable coming to her, but if it was just me, a fifty-something white male, they might not act that way."

Hayes has also built a new digital platform for diverse talent at Fox to share their stories internally; she's revamped the firm's college recruitment; she's leading a new high-potential early-career program; and she's massively increased Fox News' participation in diversity conventions, such as that of the National Association of Black Journalists.

"We now have a substantial number of our leaders attend," Hayes says of that convention, "decision makers and bureau chiefs who were recruiting on-site. And the feedback that we got from these leaders was incredible. 'I really enjoyed the fact that I felt part of something,' one told me. 'I've always gone to this conference, but I never went as a Fox person.' And I heard too from the association that participants in the convention were saying things like *Wow, did you see all the people that were over at Fox? I met this great person at Fox. I didn't even know they had opportunities there to work in roles like that.*"

So, like any good sponsor-protégé relationship, this one has boosted the careers of both parties. It is based on performance, loyalty, and that extra value that came when Lord purposefully included in his circle someone so different from himself. It is also the result of these two talented people consciously investing in each other over the years.

"We've listened to the things that matter to each other and found ways in which we could add value to one another by leveraging the resources that we have, providing access to the people and resources that we've accumulated over time," Hayes says. "It's been really reciprocal in that way."

Add a "New Muscle" to Leadership

We met Tiger Tyagarajan, CEO of Genpact, in chapter 3, where we looked at the payoffs that Saj, one of his longtime protégés has given him. Recently he took on someone new—and a big part of why he chose her is that her leadership style is so different from his.

The position Tyagarajan was looking to fill was very senior: a new chief strategy officer. Besides seeking out a top performer, he also wanted to use this hire to further two business imperatives: deepening and broadening his leadership team with a different approach and perspective; and giving Genpact a richer pool of top female talent.

Tyagarajan was proud of his top team, but he had noticed that two leadership types were dominant. "One is the executive who thinks, *I know the answer, so let's duke it out,*" Tyagarajan says. "Most of the time he's not even listening, but he's loving the fight, speaking loud even if he drowns out other voices. The second is the executive who thinks, *I have a view but it's tough to express, so I'm going to sit back, and unless something comes up that deeply impacts me, I'm not going to get into this discussion.*

"These guys do great jobs, but I wanted to add a new muscle. A good listener who has a strong point of view. Someone who's stubborn around expertise and values, but is also willing to mold views based on new information and discussion."

Women are more likely, Tyagarajan believed, to have that different style that he wanted, and even though his senior leadership team already had several women, he wanted more. "If there are just a few people who are different, they tend to go with the flow and try to blend in. You need a critical mass of women at the top before you really feel a difference," he says.

Another woman in senior leadership would bring a further advantage. Genpact's business depends on recruiting and retaining top talent, especially in technology, and a significant proportion of that talent is female. So, under Tyagarajan's leadership, Genpact has started multiple initiatives for women, such as a program to help mothers stay in the workforce and another to help senior women who've taken a career break return to a high-level job.[2]

Such initiatives are stronger when there are role models to support them. The best way to prove that there's no glass ceiling is if it's already been broken. Hiring another woman into top management would send that message powerfully.

After months of searching, Tyagarajan landed on Katie Stein—who brought with her a superlative résumé, with skills honed at the highest levels of the Boston Consulting Group and Mercer. Three months after Stein joined Genpact, Tyagarajan assigned her to present strategy at the firm's annual investor day. She knocked it out of the park, using the "muscle" that he'd sought.

"I would be thumping the table and saying, 'This is what we're going to do and this is the reason,'" he says. "She was understated, but specific, clear, and crisp. Afterward one of our biggest investors came up and said, 'Where'd you find her? She was great!' Then my chairman came to me and said, 'She did a fabulous job.'"

Skilled sponsor that he is, Tyagarajan had worked hard to set Stein up for this success: blocking out time to meet with her, providing external coaching and other resources to support her, setting up "checkpoints" with the board for her ahead of the investor day, and advising her on handling certain individuals. And since this relationship is quite new, he was also keeping a close eye on her ability to absorb guidance.

So far, so good, and Tyagarajan is optimistic that the ways in which she's different from most of top leadership—including himself—will deliver benefits beyond her specific role.

"By choosing a person with a different personality and leadership style, you make other people realize that you don't need to be a bull in the china shop to be successful. They see that you can be collaborative and get things done, achieve your goals, without having to just double down on those things that you think you believe in. You can be open to testing your knowledge and beliefs."

Tyagarajan is also confident that hiring her has helped strengthen his other initiatives to make Genpact an employer of choice for talented, ambitious women.

"I wouldn't be surprised if five years from now, half my team are women," he says. "It's very possible. In fact I'd be shocked if it didn't happen."

Fill Knowledge Gaps

When in 2016 Eileen Taylor became head of global regulatory management for Deutsche Bank, she needed a top team on the ground,
in many countries around the world. But in Deutsche's home market,
Germany, the head of the local team left soon after Taylor took up the
reins. She was faced with finding someone she could trust who also
knew German banking regulations inside and out. Her own career
had been in New York and London, and she doesn't speak German—
both complicating factors.

"I believe in a transparent hiring process," she says, "not just tap-
ping your network. So I posted the role, I interviewed applicants, and
although none of them excited me, I was on the verge of hiring one.
Then someone in HR called me and said, 'Do you know Friedrich
Stroedter? If not, meet him.'"

Taylor didn't have time to meet in person with Stroedter, who was
already at Deutsche Bank in a different position. But they had a video
call, where the depth of his country-specific knowledge and the strength
of his local contacts—neither of which she had—blew her away.

She made him head of the unit and asked him to restructure it, an
especially challenging task in Germany. "German employment law is
strict and labor unions are powerful," Taylor says. "But Friedrich has
the knowledge of German labor laws to get all that done, while at the
same time, he's up to date on all the regulatory issues. He'll tell me,
under German stock exchange rules, that when so-and-so happens,
we have to make a public statement in this way, tell the regulators
in this manner, and here are the people we need to contact to get it
done."

To show her gratitude and strengthen his commitment to her and
her team, Taylor then to bat for Stroedter. "I went on a big campaign

to get him a raise. In a tough year for us, when no one was getting raises or bonuses, I got him a big salary hike, twenty percent. When I told him, his mind was blown." But she did not stop there.

When Stroedter faced pressure from senior management, Taylor defended him. "I wrote a long, detailed email explaining how well he was doing," she says. She had to write on his behalf, because his understated, introverted manner makes him at times poorly equipped to toot his own horn.

"I do things for him, just as he does so much for me," she says.

It's that kind of reciprocity—not just in effort, but also in complementary skill sets and backgrounds—that helps make sponsorship so powerful. In the playbook's next step, we'll look at how sponsors can raise the odds that this reciprocity will truly come to be.

Breaking It Down

When you're looking for potential protégés, it's tempting to home in on those people that remind us of ourselves—whether it's in their communication and leadership style, looks, knowledge, or experience. But you can get much more out of the relationship if you include people of different backgrounds, ethnicities, gender, education, and perspectives. Here are a few tips to keep in mind as you strive for inclusivity.

- **Seek out diversity deliberately.** Unless your networks are different from that of most Americans, odds are, if you don't make a conscious effort, all your protégés will be mini-me's. Keep Ed Gilligan's one-plus-two rule in mind: two of your three protégés should be different from you in some important way.

- **Look at all dimensions of diversity.** Some kinds of diversity, such as gender and race, are inherent. Others, such as tech skills, fluency in foreign languages, or social media savvy, are acquired.[3] Keep both kinds in mind as you seek to fill gaps in the skills that you have and the perspectives and experiences to which you have access. The ideal pick may provide both kinds: Marsheila Hayes provided Kevin Lord with both inherent diversity, as a black woman, and acquired diversity, with the tech skills and social media savvy she brought to the table.

- **Mobilize all your networks.** When selecting a protégé, some leaders like Kenji Yoshino turn to proven performers at their current place of work. Other leaders, like Kevin Lord, reach out to young talent they helped develop at a previous place of work. And yet others instigate an arms-length search. Tiger Tyagarajan was looking for a different leadership style than that on offer at Genpact, so when he was seeking a new chief marketing officer he looked externally. The guideline here is to "mix and match" all three approaches and be prepared, like Kevin Lord, to reach several levels below yourself on the corporate ladder.

6

Inspire for Performance and Loyalty

In step one of the playbook, we looked at how top leaders identify potential protégés: the qualities successful sponsors look for in protégés, and the processes they use to find them. In step two I made the case for *inclusion*. When sponsors reach across the divides of gender, generation, and culture to find high-performing protégés with different identities, experiences, and skills, they win big—and their organizations do too.

We now turn to the next steps. After you've identified a diverse portfolio of protégés, how do you develop your picks? How do you *inspire* them with your vision and ignite their ambition, expanding their dreams of what they can accomplish on your team? And how do you *instruct* them, giving them the feedback that will allow them to grow the hard and soft skill sets that will make them star players on the team?

One step is to invite your protégé into your world in ways that are not risky and do not run into the head winds of the #MeToo movement. To create bonds with protégés, sponsors in our survey report inviting them to breakfast or lunch (41 percent), setting aside time to learn about their family (41 percent), sharing stories of their own early challenges or struggles (38 percent), and revealing personal information about themselves (37 percent).

Another key step is to encourage protégés to dream big for themselves and their role in your organization. Forty percent of sponsors in our survey said that they've boosted their protégés' ambition, and 38 percent said they helped them develop a career vision. Protégés who aren't receiving that kind of support are less motivated: 50 percent of protégés overall said that if their sponsor helped them shape their vision for their career, they'd be more loyal to that sponsor.

Inspiration needs to come before instruction. High-performing talent is more likely to accept unvarnished feedback and knuckle down, if you've first inspired passion and commitment. Inspiration lights up the brain, fires up energy, and raises the odds that you'll be investing in someone who won't take their new skills elsewhere but will invest back in you.

Let's now look at how two leaders in two very different fields—healthcare and advertising—inspire protégés.

Communicate the Mission

Karen Lynch, the first woman president of managed healthcare giant Aetna, is a leader with a mission. "I want to make the healthcare system a lot easier than it is today," she says, "I want people to have access to the care they need, and the education they need on how to navigate the system. I have a passion for making a difference, and as a company, we do amazing things for people."

But managed healthcare giants like Aetna aren't always seen so positively. Therefore, one of the things Lynch looks for in protégés—and looks to cultivate in them—is a shared sense of this mission to help and the ability to communicate this mission to others, inside and outside the enterprise.

Her eye for spotting this kind of passion for better access and education, joined with talent and determination, led her to a young woman whom we'll call Emma.

"I was doing site visits," Lynch says, "and I heard Emma present her vision in her market, which was a very small market. I saw that she understood all the levers of the business. She understood the competitive landscape. She understood how the company makes money, and she had ideas about how she could mold her business and propel it forward. And then I saw something else too.

"Her dad was struggling with his health, and he was challenged with the healthcare system. And she was not afraid to talk about it, in a business setting, with me, the president of the company, present. She took some of the struggles that her dad was having in order to say, 'Here's some of the things I think as a company we should be doing differently, and here's some of the things that I'm trying and that I'm piloting in my market.'"

Emma's story resonated with Lynch, who herself uses storytelling to project her vision. "When I recruit people and attempt to inspire them by what we do in the company, I often talk about two life experiences," she says. "One is my mom committing suicide when I was twelve, and how that's fueled my passion to make sure that we understand the whole person, making sure that the behavioral component is part of what we do every day, part of holistic medicine and the holistic care of an individual.

"The second is that when my mom died, my aunt looked after us. She took care of her parents too, and her husband died early in their marriage. They had one child, so she was a single mom way back when, and she took all four of us children in. She never finished high school. She and my mom were big smokers, and when my aunt was in the hospital, dying of lung cancer, and I was in my early twenties, I remember not knowing what questions to ask, not knowing anything about how to navigate this healthcare nightmare.

"I want to make sure that no one whom Aetna serves has to face that kind of confusion and hardship, that sense of being lost in the healthcare system. So when I talk about what we do every day, and why I do what I do, it's so we can help people."

Inspire by Support and Example

Having seen Emma's talent, passion, and ability to communicate that passion, Lynch did more than share her own story; she gave Emma a larger market to run, making clear that her door was always open, and expected her protégé to check in regularly.

"On a quarterly basis I would look at her results," Lynch says. "I visited her market, challenged her to make sure she was doing the right things, particularly on the people side. I wanted to make sure she had the right bench strength, the right succession, the right talent in place to support her overall success. I wouldn't say I was day-to-day hands on, but it was enough that she knew that I was invested in her and invested in her career."

She also sent Emma, and another promising young woman at Aetna, to a Harvard Business School program to develop women directors.

"She came back and said, 'Oh my god, Karen, I've never had that kind of experience. I've never been exposed to so many different industries, so many different kinds of people. Now I need to think about what my plan is over the course of the next several years as I ready myself to serve on a board.'"

These steps are clearly big moves for boosting Emma's ambition and her vision for where her career can go. But Lynch also wants to make sure that Emma, like her other trusted protégés, finds purpose and passion in Aetna's larger goals.

"The biggest trend in healthcare is moving to a much more con-sumer-focused, retail-oriented business, and it's not lost on us that all healthcare is local," Lynch says. "So I want up and coming leaders to be part of the communities where we work. I always say, 'I think you should consider a nonprofit board, and pick something you're passion-ate about so you're committed.' Our goal is to improve the health of individuals' lives, one person, one community, one nation at a time. And if we don't have our people in their communities, being part of it, being on these boards, having civic responsibility, then we're not going to make the differences we need to make."

Emma didn't need to be asked twice; she jumped at the opportu-nity to work on the board of a nonprofit in her community. And since, as Lynch says, "it's all about action, it's not about words," Lynch leads through example. She's active in several nonprofits, including Susan G. Komen, which is working for a cure for breast cancer; NEADS, which provides service dogs for disabled Americans; and the Bushnell Center for the Performing Arts in Hartford, the community where Aetna has its headquarters.

Inspiration by example extends to how Lynch acts inside the com-pany too. "Every time that I get an email from a customer, I personally respond," she says. "The people that work for me, they see that, and it shows that I'm committed to making a difference. I always say, 'These people that are reaching out to us, they have brothers, sisters, family members, just like you and I. So let's make sure that we're treating them that way.' Saying those words is one thing, but once they see it in action, that's another part of the story that helps inspire them. It makes them think about doing things differently."

Emma, meanwhile, has done phenomenally well. In the first stretch assignment that Lynch gave her, "she grew the top line and the bottom line. She turned the leadership around. And subsequent to that, we've given her more and more responsibilities, and now she's running one of the largest markets in the company."

Lynch's inspirational support has been there for Emma in tough times as well as good. A few months ago when Lynch, buoyed up by Emma's stellar performance, put her in front of Aetna's CEO, her protégé stumbled. Emma started well, successfully outlining her strategy, presenting back-up evidence, and mapping out the resources she needed, but she got flustered when the CEO challenged her on some key points of her strategic vision. She couldn't respond convincingly.

"I gave her some really tough feedback," Lynch says. "I said 'When you go in to talk to a CEO there are some big questions you need to be ready for and you weren't prepared. I expect you to rework your presentation and make it iron clad—and I'm going to help you.' The next day I gave her the budget to hire consultants to figure out how precisely to risk-proof her strategic plan. I asked her to send her reworked strategy to the CEO with a note of thanks for the valuable feedback."

That kind of support is highly inspirational: you've messed up in front of your sponsor's boss, and instead of punishing you, she doubles down and gives you the resources to do better next time. Lynch reports that Emma emerged from this experience more determined than ever to bring her passion—and Lynch's passion—for better, more accessible healthcare into her everyday work.

Inspire through Empowerment

When Michael Roth became chairman and CEO of advertising giant Interpublic Group (IPG) in 2005, one of his goals was to position the firm to serve the US and global markets as they actually were: diverse. "At the time, IPG was nowhere on diversity," he says. "It was all white males, and we had to do something about that. From a business point of view, we had to pay attention to what the world was really like."

IPG had a chief diversity officer, an African American woman named Heide Gardner. But she was, Roth says, "window dressing, and she knew it." Roth noted Gardner's impressive résumé, met with her several times to learn about her programs and ideas, then decided to get personally involved on her behalf. He met with the heads of IPG's various brands and divisions.

"I told them that diversity was going to be part of our DNA, that we were going to have to make changes, I'm going to hold you accountable making them, and Heide is in charge of this. She'll work with you, she'll have programs, and she reports to me directly. When she says, 'We need to do this,' think of it as me telling you, 'You need to do this.'"

That kind of empowerment makes a huge difference—neither Gardner nor anyone else at IPG would now think of her as merely "window dressing." Gardner could make big plans for her role in transforming the organization and count on support, especially since she and Roth worked together to link formal inclusion scorecards with executive incentives. When this new linkage led to some pushback, Roth backed her up, just as he'd promised.

"I had a CEO of one of the smaller units who failed his inclusion scorecard," Roth recalls. "In fact, he was negative. So I cut his bonus by $150,000. He called up, threatened to quit and take his clients with him. And I said to him, 'At the beginning of the year I gave you objectives, you knew them, and you failed at them. If it was a financial goal and you didn't deliver, you'd understand you wouldn't get paid, right?' He said yes. I said, 'Consider this the equivalent of a financial result. Next year, if you do better and meet the result, you'll get that bonus.'"

Roth made sure that Gardner knew about this conversation, and many others. She sends him three or four emails a day, he says, and he always responds, sometimes with personal stories. "I told her something that happened when I was head of another firm. One of my agents, an African American man, called me up and said, 'Have you been to the Washington office?' I hadn't. 'Do me a favor and go,' he said. 'Why?' I asked. 'Just go,' he said. 'Trust me on this one.'

"I went down to DC, I asked around, and I found out that the head of that office belonged to the Klan. He was a top performer, but it didn't matter. I fired him on the spot."

Roth's belief in Gardner and her mission goes far beyond words. Decisive supporting actions are a great way to make a protégé feel valued and to inspire loyalty. But not all protégés come as fully pre-pared as Gardner did. Often, as we'll see in chapter 7, you'll need to help them develop and deploy the skills they need so that they—and you—can shine.

Breaking It Down

Sponsor-protégé relationships begin with aligning passion and ambi-tion. If you can inspire a protégé with a vision of what you can achieve together, he or she will be more committed and better prepared to go the extra mile for you. The following tips will help you create align-ment, and deepen the likelihood of a joined journey.

- **Look inward and unpack your own motivations and drive**. What keeps you committed and contributing to your career and orga-nization? Is it your personal compensation and chance at pro-motion? Seeing the enterprise's bottom line and global footprint grow? Or perhaps it's a collaborative corporate culture, or the allure of being in a company that is on the cutting edge of AI or healthcare and that will transform all our lives? Whatever the answer is, start with what inspires you.

- **Use this knowledge to align with and fire up a protégé—or potential protégé**. You don't have to be an orator to inspire. You have to come from a place of authenticity and conviction. If you can't fire up a protégé with your values and goals, you probably have the wrong pick.

- **Walk the walk**. Whether it's Michael Roth showing zero tolerance for racism, or Karen Lynch personally responding to consumer emails, inspirational leaders act on their ideals. A protégé is more likely to follow you if they see you practicing what you preach.

- **Listen**. Although protégés should do most of the work, and you will reap significant benefits for the relationship, it's not all about you. Make sure you understand what your protégé values and—if those values align with yours—make sure that you respect them. It was through listening that Karen Lynch both found Emma and saw the best ways to provide inspirational support.

7

Instruct to Fill the Gaps

Horacio Rozanski and Tiger Tyagarajan, whom we met earlier in this book, sponsored individuals who already had superb skills. They chose these protégés precisely because they were ready to deliver performance and a value add at the highest levels.

But there's another common scenario: talented protégés who lack a few key skills, whether professional or interpersonal. They need a sponsor who won't just believe in their value and have their back. They need a sponsor who will work to help them grow into their potential.

It's one of the many ways in which sponsors deliver for their protégés, so that these protégés in turn are better able to support them and their organizations. According to CTI's survey, 74 percent of sponsors give their protégés career advice, 64 percent provide specific, concrete feedback, and 40 percent boost their protégés' ambition. It only makes sense: you want your protégé to choose the right path, to become better at what they do, and to rise with you.

To see how that works in practice, let's take a look at two senior executives in two different business sectors. One, already at the pinnacle of his career, sponsored a young woman near the start of hers. The other sponsored an industry veteran older than herself who nonetheless had gaps in her skill set.

Both, as we'll see, crossed lines of difference, took similar high-impact approaches toward instructing protégés, and in doing so, reaped significant rewards for themselves personally and for their organization.

Help a Protégé Find a Unique Value Proposition

Kent Gardiner is one of the nation's leading litigators and antitrust attorneys. For nearly ten years he was chair of the law firm Crowell & Moring. During his tenure the firm doubled in size, and Law360 named him to its list of "innovative managing partners." He also helped initiate the firm's first sponsorship efforts and has been a steadfast champion of women. He appointed the first woman managing partner, for example, and pushed to increase the female membership of the management board to more than 40 percent.

He has since stepped back from chairing the firm—making sure, before he stepped away, to position one of the most successful female partners to succeed him. He also remains a member of the firm's management board and chairs its litigation and trial department. A former US Department of Justice trial attorney, he has represented some of the world's biggest companies, including (in recent years) DuPont and several major global airline companies.

Given Gardiner's stature, hundreds of young lawyers would seize the chance to be his protégé. But when Gardiner stepped down he had a particular vision for how he wanted to contribute. To start with, he was looking to enrich his life at this juncture in his career. "I didn't need clients. I didn't need money," he explained. "What I did want was to be better . . . just to be a deeper person." He also wanted to help his firm in a critical area: diversity. So when a peer suggested that he sponsor a young black woman who'd recently made partner but was struggling to showcase her particular talents, he was intrigued.

"This young woman was talented but suffered from an extraordinary level of invisibility," he explained, "both inside the firm and with clients."

This woman, whom we'll call Sonia, was seen as having a valuable but somewhat generic set of legal skills in the area of employment law. But as Gardiner would soon discover, that was not due to a lack of ambition or talent, but to a personality trait. Sonia was incredibly shy. That made it hard for her to jockey for position within the firm and it limited her networking opportunities outside of it.

One of the things that makes Gardiner such a good sponsor is that he's not only eager to cross lines of difference, he's also willing to respect those differences and use them to his organization's advantage. "It's usually not a good idea to tell a protégé, 'Be more forceful.' That just means: be more like me," he explains. "I try to tailor my advice to them. They have to find their own comfort zone, their own unique way of projecting strength."

For example, a trial lawyer needs executive presence, but that can come in many forms. A tall man, like Gardiner, may simply stand up and speak emphatically. But, he says, "a top trial lawyer in the firm, a five-foot-one woman, very powerful, never stands behind a podium, which would almost entirely hide her from view. She steps forward and engages the jury directly."

With Gardiner's new protégé, her problem wasn't a lack of legal skills. "She was a superb lawyer already," he says. "That's why she made partner and that's why a peer brought her to my attention. But she had to learn to present herself more effectively."

From Whiteboard to Marketplace

Gardiner began his work with Sonia by setting up monthly meetings in an office with a big whiteboard on the wall.

"What's special about you?" he asked her.

"Nothing," she said timidly. "I'm just one of many lawyers in this practice."

Given what he'd heard about her skills, Gardiner suspected that this response was really just humility or self-doubt. He set out to find out where her special talents lay, the ones that would not only add value to the firm and its clients, but would also bolster this young woman's confidence.

He wrote a number of focus areas on the whiteboard and probed her with questions. Faced with this grilling, Sonia found she was able to push back and come up with new ideas, particularly on work she had done handling sensitive matters for government contractors involving industry-specific laws and regulations. Despite her modesty, she recognized what Gardiner had drawn out in her: she was remarkably knowledgeable on these topics. With her expertise in this area, she could add more value to the firm than her peers could, and she could begin to build a reputation.

"That transformed her attitude about her own legitimacy," Gardiner told me. "She realized that she belonged."

The monthly whiteboarding sessions didn't stop there. "Once we figured out her value proposition, we could go to work on presentation of self," Gardiner said. "How do you brand yourself? How do you come to be thought of as a player inside your value proposition? She had to understand the impact of a particular way of presenting herself to a particular constituency. And she couldn't do it as I would. She had to find her own way."

Together, they discussed what kind of writing she could do to establish her name in this field, what kind of clients would be most receptive to her, and how she could talk to them.

That process took three whiteboarding sessions. Then he was ready to take her into the marketplace. He chose the first meeting carefully: clients who both needed her particular skill set and with whom—given her shyness—she could communicate her expertise quietly.

Now, many such meetings later, Gardiner and Sonia simply swap notes. He rarely gives her feedback on legal matters, since she's an unusually adept lawyer. Instead, he might mention a moment where she could have spoken up, or how she might create an opportunity to do so next time.

It's been four years since Gardiner first started sponsoring Sonia. "Her economic value to the firm has increased significantly," he says. "Clients are coming to us to hire her specifically now." As a result, her compensation has grown. "And something else has begun to grow too: her confidence," Gardiner adds. "Her success with clients has encouraged her to be more assertive with her good ideas internally, and something of a buzz has developed around her. She is now thought of as on a track toward leadership roles in the firm. And she is enjoying it."

Along the way, Gardiner satisfied one of his own goals in sponsorship: to broaden his awareness and grow as a person. "What she has been teaching me, without even knowing it, is that when you get to differences as wide as race, you're dealing with far more than opportunity. You're dealing literally with the human experience of how to be in a community and feel like you belong. And so I had to go way, way down to the basics of that understanding to be effective across the racial divide." Beyond helping Sonia and the firm, which was satisfying in its own right, Gardiner also acquired valuable insight—and experience—by viewing the world through a very different set of eyes. "Before you get to legacy," he says, "you have to live better."

Make a Plan

Jacqueline Welch is head of HR at mortgage giant Freddie Mac, but ten years ago, she was an SVP at Turner Broadcasting System, the parent of CNN and half a dozen other television networks. There she had an administrative assistant who "clearly and evidently could do more."

So one day Welch asked her, "If you could do anything, what would you want to do?" This young woman, whom we'll call Rita, had a highly specific answer: talent acquisition. Welch recalls that Rita even gave the example of a woman "we both knew who worked in talent acquisition and said, 'I want to be like her.' It was a big reach. She didn't have the academic background."

But, from working with her daily, Welch was already convinced that Rita had extraordinary talent and drive. "So we sat down and talked: Getting from here to there, what does that look like? What do you need to know? Who can teach you? Who do you need to know? What are the exposures? Are there projects you can get on to get visibility and experience? We sat side by side, wrote down everything that we thought needed to happen, and then we timeboxed.

"We made lists of the recruiters that I had a relationship with, and she went around and started talking to people, it was one of the tasks I gave her: go talk to a certain number of recruiters at Turner and find out their career trajectory. How did they become who they are? Then she came back and we unpacked the stories and talked about the skill sets she needed and what she already had that sounded a lot like what these people had.

"Then there were opportunities on projects which did not seem open to administrative assistants like her, but I told her to go say she wanted to be a part of one of these projects. It will be in addition to your job, I told her, but it will give you some exposure and give you a sense of how things work. And when I could, I would tip the scales in her favor and say, 'You know, I know it's not the most traditional thing, but she's got the chops. Let her on the project.'

"And she was patient. This was not a woman who thought anything would happen for her overnight or be given to her on a silver platter. She had grit and did the work. It took years, but she stayed with it, she stuck to the plan. Now she's a recruiter for CNN. She managed to make that difficult transition within a company from administrative assistant to the management ranks."

Instruct through Structure

Gardiner and Welch found their protégés the way many leaders do: through personal connections or a peer's recommendation. But many forward-thinking large companies are formalizing the sponsorship process. That has a lot to recommend it—and I do recommend it—but it's still up to the two people involved to make the relationship work, and to make it last past the program's end point.

Cassandra Frangos knows all about sponsorship programs. As vice president for global executive talent—the chief talent officer—at Cisco, she helped design one. Even so, her own personal sponsorship experience came about largely through a protégé's initiative.

In 2010, Frangos was leading Cisco's Executive Action Learning Forum (E-ALF). E-ALF selected promising executives, put them in teams of ten, and assigned each team a major business problem. Solving for each of these problems could mean at least $1 billion in revenue for Cisco.

That year, before she'd assigned the E-ALF participants to their teams, Frangos gave her usual orientation speech. Afterward, a marketing executive whom we'll call Diane came up to her. Diane wasn't exactly a newcomer in the corporate world. She was, Frangos later learned, older than she was, and she had several decades of work experience under her belt. She nonetheless displayed an impressive level of fresh energy and eagerness.

"Feel free to assign me to the hardest time zone, the most complex geography," Diane told Frangos. "Even if I have to work crazy night hours, I don't care, I want to learn."

The E-ALF program was in part a competition, so participants didn't usually ask if they could start with a particularly difficult task. Diane's unusual suggestion piqued Frangos's attention. She went ahead and assigned her to a team working on the Indonesia market. That obliged Diane to keep Indonesian hours—which meant working in the middle of the night—and to pick up country specific knowledge from scratch. At the assignment's start, she didn't know a thing about Indonesia or the technology marketplace there.

There was another reason why Frangos took note of Diane: a senior executive of Cisco had come up to Frangos, identified himself as Diane's boss, and said, "Diane's very, very good. Keep an eye on her."

There was a third reason too why Frangos paid special attention to Diane: Diane is African American, and as is the case in many companies, black women are underrepresented in executive ranks at Cisco.

"That was a bonus," Frangos told me. "I was certainly going to be happy to see an African American woman do well. But the big reasons why I paid attention to her were what I heard from the business and what I saw about her own attitude."

In E-ALF, participants all had a senior executive as their coach, with several high-potential junior talents assigned to each coach. These coaches observed these potential protégés (called trainees at Cisco) in meetings, provided feedback on their work, and talked further in one-on-one sessions about strengths and weaknesses. At the end of the program, the coaches worked with their protégés to develop a personal development plan for each.

The program assigned trainees to coaches randomly, and it happened that Diane was assigned to Frangos. Diane continued with her bring-it-on attitude and exceptional appetite for hard work and risk. She was also eager to improve her skill sets.

The two of them came up with two areas, a concrete skill set and a more subtle leadership attribute, where Diane needed work. For example, she had trouble getting others to buy into her ideas. She tended to battle openly and passionately for her ideas. Sometimes this was appropriate, other times it would have been better if she had been more diplomatic, indirect, and done more listening.

"Diane wasn't using any finesse," Frangos told me. "She became over-passionate, riled up, her voice became hectoring, and everyone in the room started to shut down and tune out."

Frangos pointed this out—and Diane took the harsh feedback beautifully. "Oh my God," she said. "Am I going there again? I couldn't hear myself. I'll do better." Which she did.

That kind of attitude helped Frangos feel confident as she worked with Diane on a structured development plan. Together, they wrote down a step-by-step outline for where Diane wanted to be in a few years and how she might get there.

Advise as Needed

With that development plan, the E-ALF program was over for the year, and with it—on paper—the relationship between Frangos and Diane. But Diane decided to keep it going.

The two had gotten along well, and now, when Diane was in Frangos's city, she'd call her up and they'd go out for a meal. As the friendship grew, Frangos began to call her too, just to say hi and chat.

Diane would also call Frangos for advice: Who do I ask to help me here? How should I handle this important situation or person? I want this assignment—can you tell me who I should start networking with?

It's important to emphasize: in the sponsor-protégé relationship, it's the protégé who should be doing the heavy lifting, including being proactive in seeking feedback and instruction. Whether it's at the start, in creating a formal development plan, or later, when a protégé just needs an occasional tip or nudge, it's the protégé who should reach out and get the ball rolling.

For example, once Diane was working on a very big deal—so big that it attracted the CEO's attention and led him to work directly with her, bypassing the multiple layers of management in between. The deal went through, but several people in those middle layers of management resented that Diane had cut them out. One in particular, a very powerful man, was furious.

Diane called Frangos, who gave her tips about how to smooth ruffled feathers, and advice on how to better navigate the powerful egos at the top of any organization so as to avoid a repeat. "She could have handled it better," Frangos says, "and after we talked, I knew that next time she would."

Frangos continued to give advice and feedback and when, a year later, a position for vice-president of strategy in an engineering division opened up, she saw a chance to make a big thing happen for her protégé.

"The engineering team told me that they were willing to look at a different kind of candidate and I knew Diane was ready for a new challenge. So I told her about the opportunity and advised her strongly to apply for it."

It was a competitive process, with other candidates up for the post. But Diane won the position—which is when the hard work really began. "She had to learn a whole lot about engineering on the job," Frangos said. "She was really just thrown into the fire, and she met real resistance. Her new team was in shock: an African American woman, almost fifty years old, with a career in marketing and no engineering background! Her appointment was really a stretch for everyone."

But just as Diane had once worked late hours and learned about Indonesia to make her team a success in the E-ALF program, here she learned about risk-proofing advanced technology products, about the competitive landscape for highly specialized engineering tools, and about technical bugs in final-stage product design.

"She did it, she brought it off," Frangos says in awestruck tones. "She was a success. I recently watched her present at an event for Cisco VPs and SVPs, and I could see her impress the crowd, and I was so proud of her."

Frangos didn't just feel satisfaction for Diane's sake. She and Cisco were winners too. After all, Frangos was Cisco's senior talent officer at the time. Perhaps the biggest part of her job was uncovering talent and placing it where it could best help the company prosper and grow. She was also tasked with increasing the flow of talent between technology and non-technology divisions. When that succeeds, it offers great advantages to the firm. "With her engineering experience, when Diane goes back to sales, she'll be even more effective than she was before," Frangos says. And yet another part of Frangos's job was to help women and people of color fulfill their potential within Cisco, since diversity in leadership provides several competitive advantages.[1]

"With Diane, it was a home run," Frangos says, "it was one of those business relationships that provide enormous value, a big reputation boost, and personal satisfaction for everyone involved."

So Frangos, like Gardiner, found big benefits for herself and her organization by working with a protégé who had already demonstrated talent but also had unfulfilled potential. That's only logical: in business some of the biggest profits come from seeing hidden value, then helping to bring that value to light.

But not every investment is a success. Just because you've chosen a protégé thoughtfully and are providing instruction and guidance, it doesn't mean that you assign your trust blindly. You have to keep your eyes open. If you're bringing someone new into your orbit, you need to be sure that your initial estimate of their talent and character was correct.

In the playbook's next step, we'll take a look at how to keep an eye on protégés so that you not only empower them, but also protect yourself.

Breaking It Down

No protégé is perfect. There may be gaps in their knowledge or skill set that they need to fix in order for them to truly meet your needs. Part of the sponsorship relationship is to work with your protégé to build them up. Instructing them on how to go about closing any skills gaps is part of that process. The following tips will help you take on this crucial step.

- **Make the protégé do the work**. When you consider protégés with clear gaps in their skill sets, they may need a development plan—but most of the planning should be done by the protégé. A great early assignment for potential protégés is to identify three skills gaps and the steps they intend to take to close those gaps. Offer feedback on their plan and perhaps one piece of targeted coaching, but make clear that they must own their own development.

- **Become less formal over time**. As protégés advance in their careers, and as you become more confident in each other, their demands on you should dial back to occasional advice—with the burden on them to reach out as needed.

- **Offer unvarnished feedback.** You don't want to be cruel but you want to be honest. Take off the kid gloves and level with your protégé about shortfalls in performance or loyalty. You need to because you could be at risk. If a protégé underperforms in front of your boss (the case of Karen Lynch and Emma comes to mind), or criticizes you in front of a client, you'll need to call this out immediately because your brand could be seriously hurt.

- **Encourage your protégé to "green light" unvarnished feedback.** Especially if your protégé is a different gender or ethnicity, it's important that he or she learn to signal an appetite for critical as well as supportive feedback. Explain that you'll need their permission to provide constructive criticism so that they can grow their skill sets, but that you'll always be speaking as an ally, not an enemy. You might frame it as tough love.

8

Inspect Your Prospects

By this stage you've identified a few promising protégés—and gone out of your way to make sure that you include talent that doesn't look like you. You've worked to inspire your protégés to deliver passion as well as top-notch performance, and you've offered instruction to help them close skills gaps so they can fully realize their potential.

But sponsorship is an investment, and like any investment, you have to keep an eye on it. Are your protégés developing as you hoped, rewarding your commitment? Is it time to stay the course, make some adjustments, redouble your efforts, or even reassess your commitment? No investor gets it right every time. It's important to know when to cut your losses and move on. And although inspection is discussed in detail here, since it's a logical time—before deciding whether to ramp up your commitment to in a prospective protégé—some kind of inspection should be occurring throughout the relationship, from the start to its maturity. It's tempting to think that after you've known someone a few years, you can put the relationship on autopilot, but that's often unwise.

In CTI's survey, we asked sponsors what would signal they should end a relationship with a protégé. The top signal, which 73 percent cited, was a lack of loyalty, displayed by protégés who bad-mouthed them, damaged their reputation, or had undermined their trust in some other way.

Trevor Phillips, for example, remembers a protégé who "thought my sponsorship gave her permission not to have to do the job. She thought it was enough for her to tell people, 'Trevor has said this. You must do it.' And then she didn't do the work herself. She arrogated my authority and abused it. So I fired her."

After loyalty issues, the second biggest signal for severing a relationship with a protégé (56 percent) was performance concerns, which included protégés who made too many mistakes, didn't live up to expectations, or needed too much oversight. Sponsorship shouldn't be hard work, it should be the protégé who does the heavy lifting: letting you know about skills gaps or difficulties on the job and reaching out to you for instruction or advice.

Let your prospective protégé know that it's their responsibility to find touch points that don't burden you excessively. "Let's grab a quick breakfast tomorrow morning," he or she might suggest, having checked your calendar and made sure that you will be in the office early. Or they might reach out with a suggestion: "I see we're both going to that company offsite on Friday. I'd love to drive together: it would give us a chance to get caught up. I'd be happy to swing by your house to pick you up if that makes it easier."

But if you find that you're the one who always has to reach out, or if they reach out so much that they are a burden, then it's time to first instruct them as to your expectations, and then, if that fails, consider removing them from your pool of protégés.

Sponsors also cited low ambition (51 percent), failing to work well with a team (50 percent), and not acting on feedback (32 percent) as signals that they should terminate a sponsor-protégé relationship.

Other than disloyalty, which is a red flag that suggests you should immediately severe the relationship, these problems don't offer easy answers. If someone isn't performing as expected, is it time to terminate the relationship, or to provide more guidance? If they lack ambition, could you spark it? Maybe they can learn to do teamwork better. Perhaps you could express feedback more clearly. Or maybe you really do have to end things. Making this decision is incredibly complex, and the examples in this chapter provide a few different ways to respond.

Of course, inspection of your protégé shouldn't always turn up problems. Hopefully you'll discover achievement and payoff—signs that you should continue with your alliance. Some common things that sponsors in our survey say their primary protégés have done for them include:

- Going the extra mile (54 percent)

- Performance that makes the sponsor look good (44 percent)

- Building the sponsor's brand as someone who picks and nurtures great talent (38 percent)

- Lightening the sponsor's workload by taking on responsibilities (37 percent)

- Giving the sponsor honest, critical feedback (32 percent)

- Leading with a yes (30 percent)

With that data in mind, let's take a look at how three highly successful executives inspected their protégés and reacted to what they found—both good and bad.

Rewarding a Protégé Who Delivers

Michael Roth, chairman and CEO of advertising giant Interpublic Group (IPG), empowered and inspired Heide Gardner as part of his successful quest to make IPG better able to win talent and business in a diverse and global marketplace.

Gardner is just one instance of how sponsoring has played a role in Roth's remarkable career. Currently, he's keeping an eye on a protégé who's done so well that he's a strong candidate to succeed Roth at the helm when he retires.

The first meeting with this future protégé was dramatic. Before he became chairman and CEO, Roth was on IPG's board and was attending a board meeting when a young man burst in. He asked the board members to stop what they were doing and listen to him.

"I said, 'Who is this guy, interrupting us?' It turned out he was the person who dealt with reporters, the communications guy for IPG, Philippe Krakowsky. He was coming to tell us that he'd been on the phone with the press, and reporters had the story that we were discussing at that very board meeting. And they were calling Philippe for comments. So he thought he'd better come and tell us there was a leak out there about the very thing we were discussing. 'This is why I'm here to talk to you,' he said. 'This is how the press thinks you're going to vote.'

"He handled himself very well at that board meeting," Roth says. "Obviously the press felt very comfortable talking to him directly, the board was comfortable with him, and he'd made the right choice to interrupt us. So he'd covered two difficult constituencies, the press and the board, very well."

That was the beginning of Roth's identification of Krakowsky as a possible protégé. As time went on, he realized that Krakowsky, talented as he was with communications, had the potential for more. "He has an enormous capability of relating to people, whether they be high-level or starting out. He can talk to them, really tell them what they have to know, what's going on, and do it straightforwardly and diplomatically."

When Roth became IPG's chairman and CEO, he learned to value Krakowsky even more. "I was coming in and didn't know much about the industry or the organization. I did know something because I was on the board, but I wasn't in the bowels of IPG. I needed someone to help me navigate through this crazy group of people. Philippe did that."

It turned out, Roth wasn't the only one Krakowsky was helping this way. "When it came time for me to form my leadership team, what was clear to me was that everybody at IPG would call him for advice, everyone would call him to say, 'How should I approach this situation?'"

So Roth decided to give Krakowsky a chance to apply his people skills to more than the firm's PR. "We had this person running HR here, a buttoned-up guy from another company, I inherited him, I didn't hire him, and he didn't belong. I went to the board and said I'm going to replace the head of HR. They said, 'With who?' I said Philippe. People looked at me nervously. He didn't have HR experience, and I said that's why I want him.

"My entire career," Roth adds, "I've picked people who are in different jobs and switched them up. I only go for talent and smarts. I don't care about their background, I don't care what school they went to."

So Krakowsky became head of HR, an especially important role at IPG just then, because its talent was under siege.

"We had financial control issues then," Roth recalls, "which frankly is why I became the CEO. We had to deal with getting our books and records correct. We actually stopped issuing financial statements until we fixed the control issue. And at the same time, we had to run a business, so HR was very important because people were nervous we were going out of business. And we were nervous as to whether they would go work for other companies, because IPG's financial results were down and everybody else's were up."

As Roth watched closely, since these matters were so critical to IPG, Krakowsky did the job: retaining the talent IPG needed, hiring and promoting others, and also helping keep clients confident that the firm was going to be just fine. With Krakowsky having proven performance and loyalty in his new role, Roth began to prepare his protégé for even bigger things.

"Because of his success and his intelligence, I gave him another responsibility, chief strategy officer," Roth says. "He didn't have direct experience there either, but he learned fast. Part of my role is to make sure I have a successor, and I was shaping Philippe as one of the key candidates, so I had to give him operating experience. He got it. He did really well."

As Roth watched, Krakowsky delivered there too, implementing major strategic actions, such as embedding digital and emerging media capabilities across IPG's portfolio, and designing integrated, cross-agency client teams. Based on Krakowsky's continued successes, Roth made him head of one of IPG's most important units, IPG Mediabrands. There he effectively managed an organization with over ten thousand employees, while strengthening the group's digital and data-driven marketing.

In this position, as in other senior positions, inspection was straightforward: Roth could easily assess whether or not Krakowsky was delivering, since his success or failure so clearly impacted the overall organization's performance. But also key to Roth's inspection was watching how others in the organization interacted with his protégé, and built bonds of trust.

"All I want to know is if someone is real, smart, accessible, and can communicate without bullshit. Philippe is like that, and those are traits, in this industry, that are hard to come by, because everyone here is a salesperson. And people within IPG know that too. They go to him unfiltered to get his advice. They trust him, they trust his advice."

Roth has seen both Krakowsky's performance—delivering in multiple roles across IPG—and witnessed the fact that not only Roth himself, but also others throughout IPG, trust him. As a result, Krakowsky is now on the short list of candidates to succeed him.

"If you look at the studies on best candidates to succeed as a CEO," Roth says, "the best source is internal, a candidate who has been groomed by the existing CEO. I moved Philippe, over fourteen years, from a communication officer, to head of HR, to head of strategy, to head of Mediabrands, to potentially being the CEO.

"He may get the job, he may not, there are other good candidates too, but it was all very intentional on my part."

It was intentionality based on inspection, since only after Krakowsky delivered and proved his trustworthiness in each role did Roth give him another, greater one.

Deciding to Terminate

Around the same time that he started to sponsor Krakowsky, Roth recruited a man, whom we'll call Myles, to run a line of business within one of IPG's units. In this role, Myles delivered in ways that were once again easy for Roth to see, since Myles was responsible for the entire line of business.

"He repositioned the offerings, he hired great talent, he was a success," Roth says. So Roth decided to make Myles head of the whole unit, even though Myles had little experience with much of the administrative and client relations work that the new role demanded.

"Look, I take bets on people," Roth says. "As I did with Philippe, I put Myles in a job he wasn't trained for. He'd done a great job where he was, and I thought he could convert that into running an entire unit. And he couldn't. It was a mistake."

It was a mistake that Roth caught quickly. He'd given Myles specific numbers to meet; he also checked in with major clients. Because he was watching closely, he soon saw that Myles wasn't delivering the numbers or handling clients well. Even worse, when Roth called him in for a talk, Myles made excuses but failed to provide a set of solutions or a detailed plan.

"He kept telling me he was going to fix it. And I gave him plenty of opportunities. But nothing changed. The numbers didn't get any better. The clients weren't any more pleased."

In this case, since Myles was so senior, Roth couldn't end the relationship without also ending Myles's employment as IPG. So he did so. Even though Myles still had the talent that Roth had seen and cultivated in him, he'd failed to live up to expectations, and he had delivered excuses and empty promises rather than real change.

Putting an End to Unacceptable Behavior

In the case of Myles, the big problem was a failure to meet his numbers, but a more frequent scenario involves a failure of soft skills. The CEO of a public relations firm in Los Angeles, whom I'll call Marty, was actually in the process of ending a sponsor-protégé relationship on the day that we had our interview.

He had been sponsoring a woman, whom I'll call Carla, for six months—ever since he'd noted her brilliance at taking ideas from the creative team, packaging them to appeal to clients, and crafting a relationship that would benefit both the agency and the client.

So Marty gave this brilliant talent a promotion. "She was already senior, but we gave her the chance to create and define a whole new department for us, running a large portfolio of clients."

Carla—as good as she was at making presentations, handling clients, and leading a small team where she was absolute boss—failed miserably at the more subtle leadership skills required to found and lead a department.

"I was giving her constant advice and coaching," Marty says. "But she couldn't handle ambiguity. She was driving the train as fast as she could, leaving others behind, trying to make everything perfect by saying, 'If you don't do it my way, you're wrong.' But to lead a department, you have to build consensus. You have to lead through influence. You have to sculpt fog."

Marty inspected Carla by talking to her subordinates, Carla's immediate boss (Marty's number two), and Carla herself. "Her boss said she was a mess. When I gently told Carla some of her boss's criticisms, Carla asked me to fire her boss. It was crazy. I tried to give her one more chance. I told her, 'I want you to go home, think about things, and write them down. Think it through rationally and calmly and write down what you want me to do.' I thought that would temper her.

"It didn't," Marty says. "The next day she filed a formal complaint about her boss with HR. So I had to have HR go in and talk to the whole team. It's become a massive pain in the neck for me."

Carla flunked several big tests of a protégé. She'd underperformed, but given that she'd only been in the role six months that wasn't an unforgivable problem. After all, Marty took on Carla as his protégé aware that he'd have to develop her and instruct her. But Carla also failed to listen to him, and compounded that mistake by making his life more difficult. Those are utterly unacceptable behaviors. Good protégés will free you up to spend *more time* doing work you love and adding value as only you can. They most definitely will *not* increase dissension in your team and drag you into messy personnel fights.

At the time we spoke, Marty still hadn't decided whether he was going to dismiss Carla from the firm or simply move her into a different position; but what he was certain about was that this talented woman was no longer his protégé. "It's wrenching," he said. "I've never had this happen before, and I've invested so much. But I've got to think about what's good for the firm. Sponsorship isn't about me helping her. It's about the two of us together helping the business."

Forgiving a Big Mistake

Another common scenario is a protégé who is neither a complete success, as Philippe Krakowsky has been for Michael Roth, nor a straightforward failure, as Myles and Carla were. Sometimes, when you inspect a protégé, you find big flaws, but you also see ways to work with them and turn the relationship around. Kent Gardiner, who we've already seen is a pro at sponsorship, tells of an example.

"There's a woman inside my practice area whom I've been sponsoring since she just joined the firm," Gardiner says. "It was a gradual, steady, and ultimately relentless process of building up her skills and introducing her to clients." It was with the latter part that this lawyer, whom we'll call Melissa, encountered problems.

"I introduced her to clients and reassured them that she would take care of them day-to-day," he says. "Then my role would winnow down to the most strategic needs they had, as opposed to the more-detailed, daily needs they had." That's exactly the sort of benefit that a protégé should provide for a sponsor. But Melissa unintentionally did the opposite.

"She had certain characteristics, a glibness, an almost snarkiness in how she communicated," Gardiner says. "She was unduly critical of lawyers at other firms, criticizing their judgment. She didn't recognize that the client had reposed a lot of trust in those other lawyers, and that the client might think, *If she's trashing other people like this, who knows what she'll say about us?* She assumed a level of intimacy with the client that she had no foundation for."

Gardiner was in touch with both the client and other people on his team, but his inspection wasn't quite close enough: he didn't realize how big the problem was until the client, citing issues with Melissa, took its business elsewhere. "She'd gotten us fired from a relationship," Gardiner says. "So I had to decide, am I going to keep trying with her?"

It's a tough decision, and one that most sponsors may face at some point with a protégé. There are no hard and fast rules—unless the protégé shows disloyalty, in which case you must walk away immediately. Gardiner balanced several factors in his decision: Melissa's grave mistake on the one hand, and her talent and ambition on the other, as well as the difficulty of what she was attempting: to become a top trial lawyer as a young woman, in a field that is dominated by older men. He also considered whether the flaw she'd displayed was fixable.

The answer, in the end, was to double down on instruction but get a little help for it. "I saw," Gardiner recalls, "that her snarkiness was because she was very insecure, even though she was monumentally talented. So I decided, 'We're just going to power through this.' But I realized, I might not be the best person to tell an insecure young woman how to deal with powerful senior men. So I got some of my colleagues, senior women with long experience, to talk to her about client boundaries."

Fifteen years later, Melissa is now a senior woman herself. "It's become a triumphant relationship," Gardiner says. "She's fabulous. She's learned her lesson, she's learned how to be a good manager of relationships. And now, thanks to her, we have a much wider client base than before."

When the Protégé Won't Change

An executive whom I'll call Roberta is now leading HR at one of the world's most important technology companies. But in her prior position, at a financial services giant, she brought in a young woman whom we'll call Tanya.

"I saw Tanya as our next superstar," Roberta says. "I'd already figured her into our succession plan." But despite her enthusiasm, Roberta kept a close eye on Tanya. Or rather, she used the eyes and ears of others to help her inspect her prospective protégé.

"I asked people on her team about her skill sets," Roberta says. "It turned out that no one would vouch for them. I asked her direct supervisors about her value add. They weren't seeing it. Everyone liked her, they said she was friendly, but the deepest relationships aren't forged at happy hour. They're formed around the trust and integrity you develop working tightly together on a project."

So Roberta called Tanya into her office to offer some advice. "I told her to ask more questions of her team and her supervisors, since she was new. When you don't ask questions, I explained, the perception is that either you don't care or you're a know-it-all. And I told her that she had to be more than just friendly. When she met with her team at the office meet-and-greets, she had to ask what they were up to so she could get her job done."

Tanya said that she understood and would do better. But when, after another three months went by, Roberta asked business leaders about Tanya, they said that she was always sitting in on their meetings but had nothing to say. Meanwhile, Tanya hadn't been reaching out to Roberta. She hadn't been proactively offering reports on her efforts and progress. She hadn't confessed that there was still a problem and hadn't asked for more ideas.

Instead, it was again Roberta who had to call in Tanya, who again said that she'd heard the message and would do better. Concerned, Roberta now decided to attend a few meetings with Tanya and introduced her, to make it easier for her to contribute. Still: nothing. As Michael Roth had experienced with Myles, Roberta began to feel that Tanya was just making excuses and not being honest with her. Besides her disappointment with her performance, Roberta now felt that she couldn't trust her.

When Tanya's first year was up, Roberta was ready to sever the relationship. And since she had hired Tanya into a position that was senior enough that it didn't leave room for too many mistakes, she dismissed her from the company.

"It was a horrible situation," Roberta says. "I'm still certain that Tanya was remarkably talented. She just somehow couldn't ask questions, couldn't ask for help when she got in over her head, couldn't speak up when she had to. Not everyone, no matter how many directives you provide, is capable of earning sponsorship."

But for those protégés who do work out (and many do quite splendidly), after you've inspired, instructed, and inspected them, it's time to make things explicit and formalize the relationship, in your eyes and in the eyes of those around you. It's time to instigate a deal.

Breaking It Down

Once you have developed a protégé—inspiring and instructing them—your job isn't done. You need to keep an eye on them and make sure they're delivering in the ways you expect, in terms of loyalty, performance, and a value add. Here's how you can inspect your protégé.

- **Listen to others**. Some kinds of inspection are obvious, and you would perform them with any subordinate: see if they're successfully performing assigned tasks or filling in identified gaps. But for a person who will be walking around with your brand on their forehead, it's important to hear how clients, colleagues, and superiors assess them too.

- **Look for values and attitude**. It's often possible for a sponsor to fill in a skills gap, whether those skills are hard (think of how Michael Roth gave Philippe Krakowsky exposure to one part of the enterprise after another) or soft (consider how Kent Gardiner helped Melissa overcome insecurity and polish her approach). But if a protégé doesn't keep you in the loop, lacks fire in the belly, expects you to do all the work, or shows any signs of disloyalty or ingratitude, it's time to cut your losses and move on.

- **Forgive a little—but not too much**. Everyone makes mistakes, and when you take on a protégé, it's common that he or she is something of a diamond in the rough; they may not be able to check all the boxes on a checklist for perfection. But your time is limited, and they must be quick and eager learners. So, even with performance or skills gaps the rule of thumb should be three strikes and you're out.

- **Fit the punishment to the crime**. If a protégé needs more help, but their talent and loyalty remain impressive, then provide that help. But if a protégé proves to have less potential than you thought, it's reasonable to downgrade the relationship to mentorship, without any consequences. It's only if your protégé turns out to be seriously untrustworthy that you need to fire him or her. If you don't have the power to do that, sever the connection as much as possible.

9

Instigate a Deal

There comes a time when you've instructed and inspected enough. It's time to make clear: you believe in this person and you expect them to deliver for you. Your advocacy and support will now be open and often spelled out explicitly.

This step involves a certain risk, since part of your own success and reputation will be on the line, and there's no shortage of public figures who've gotten it wrong. Consider how Donald Trump decided to nominate White House physician Ronny Jackson—with whom he'd reportedly developed an excellent personal relationship—to run one of the federal government's largest divisions, the Veteran Affairs Department. After aggressively and publicly defending Dr. Jackson, President Trump had to withdraw the nomination as allegations about Dr. Jackson's professional and personal conduct piled up.[1] Even knowing someone personally for over a year, as Trump knew Jackson, may not be good enough.

CTI's data shows that many sponsors do, however, move quickly. In our survey, 87 percent of sponsors said that they feel comfortable publicly advocating for a protégé either immediately or within one year. Another 10 percent feel such comfort within three years, and only 2 percent wait more than three years before they publicly commit to a protégé.

The fact is, dealmaking in the sponsor-protégé relationship is complex, and there are no hard and fast rules—except to take precautions, which I've been laying out throughout this book. Some sponsors, like IPG CEO Michael Roth, prefer to move slowly. In the case of another CEO, he moved from identifying a protégé to instigating a deal with her almost immediately—and he did it in a way that makes the odds very much in favor of this deal working out.

Instigate on Day One—under Certain Circumstances

When Genpact CEO Tiger Tyagarajan had his recently hired chief strategy officer, Katie Stein, present at the firm's investor day, that meant putting her in front of both the Board of Directors and Genpact's biggest investors. It was clear to everyone there not just that she was a top performer, but that Tyagarajan was heavily invested in her.

He'd actually instigated a deal with her even earlier, when she hadn't yet inked the contract to join Genpact. The moment came at the end of a highly rigorous vetting process by both Genpact's search committee and Tyagarajan himself, who was closely involved in the hiring process, and who was already thinking that this new hire might be not just a new member of top leadership, but also a protégé.

During the hiring process Tyagarajan held four one-on-one interviews with Stein. In these interviews he teased out not just her professional skills and philosophy but also her ambition, her capacity for long-term loyalty to Genpact, and that mix of open-mindedness and understated determination that he was seeking. He also looked for *stories*: not accomplishments, but actions and decisions that illuminated her personality.

One story Stein told him was from an earlier employer. The organization was facing a cost crunch that obliged it to cut down on expenses, including traditional team-building events. Stein saw that her team was losing morale and energy, so she decided to throw a party for them—at her house, at her own expense.

"She just brought her whole team home one evening and they had a blast," Tyagarajan says, "and it was clear the way she told the story, she wasn't complaining. She wasn't calling the corporate cost cuts wrong. She wasn't making herself out to be any kind of hero. She just said, 'I needed my team to be with me through a very difficult time, so this is what I did, and it helped.'"

So Tyagarajan had a good sense of what Stein was like as a professional and a person, and he decided to make an offer that was more than financial. As he recalls it, "I told her, 'Look, I'm bringing you into the team. I'm convinced you're going to be successful. I'm going to make sure you're successful.' She looked at me and said, 'So you're telling me that you're going to have my back to make me successful?' I said yes."

To make such a commitment so early is a calculated bet, which can offer great rewards—if you're careful. "If you make an early bet, go full in on day one, the chances of the sponsorship process yielding success can be higher," Tyagarajan says. "The clearer you are that you're making a bet on this person, normal human behavior is for you to get a response back: loyalty. But it's a bet, and it could go wrong, so it needs to be continuously tested."

As Tyagarajan said, the key to making this bet work is to continuously test—or inspect—your new protégé. These bets can be especially sensible when your protégé, like Katie Stein, is already a highly experienced executive whom you're bringing in at a senior level. With Stein's résumé, performance was pretty much a given, though Tyagarajan still worked closely with her for several months before making this bet explicit for all the world to see at Genpact's investor day.

That's the way to instigate a deal early and make it work: vet someone carefully, and inspect them closely going forward. And it's just possible with senior executives such as Katie Stein that if done right, instigating a deal quickly can, as our next example shows, support greater performance and loyalty with less experienced professionals too.

Make the Deal Explicit

As a protégé Anne Erni delivered a payoff to her sponsor Melinda Wolfe at Bloomberg. But Erni is also a skilled sponsor herself, and with one of her protégés in a previous job—at the once-great Wall Street firm Lehman Brothers—she instigated a deal quickly.

"When I was appointed chief diversity officer of Lehman Brothers," Erni recalls, "I came from the trading floor. I had a business background, and now I was leading a corporate function. It was uncharted territory for me. And I soon realized that we didn't have any good data or analytics for diversity. They had it in HR, but weren't going to share it with me. I needed someone close to me to gather data, do the analytics, and create dashboards to track progress."

She posted the job internally, and among the applicants was a young man named Aaron Blumenthal. "He was in the CFO's office, a very junior member," Erni says. "He understood data and rigor, and the way information needed to be presented to impress our CFO. But he needed focus and guidance. He didn't always know the right way to ask questions or to approach people."

And here was the thing that enabled Erni and Blumenthal to make a deal early on: along with the superb analytics skills that Erni needed, Blumenthal had an unusual degree of self-awareness. He knew what he lacked. He wanted Erni's help to get it.

"He made it very clear," Erni recalls, "that one reason he wanted to work for me was that I had come from the business and I'd worked in sales. He wanted to learn how to sell, become more commercial, better at understanding business implications. I promised to help him do that. And then, if he helped me pull together rigorous data on diversity, I would give him more exposure to the business. I was very clear: 'If you want to be a commercial salesperson someday,' I said, 'I'll help you, but you need to help me get this department in order. If you help me create this function, I'll support you in expanding your skill set and help find a role for you.'"

Erni and Blumenthal made this deal as soon she hired him, but it took well over a year before she made her sponsorship of him public. First, of course, he delivered performance. "Very early on," she says, "Aaron produced a PowerPoint deck for me in which he took basic info and spun out some visual analytics that really showed the big picture. Then he created a little white binder for me, very organized, with tabs to guide me and visuals of the data, and said, 'This is going to be our one source of truth as we go along.' He was so organized, and he was doing exactly what I needed, which was taking HR data and presenting it as a financial executive would want to see it. That was the only way we could make our case at Lehman."

Blumenthal continued to deliver for Erni in the months that followed. "I needed to build my own credibility in this role," she says, "by providing statistical proof that 1) there was a problem and 2) I was solving it. Because Aaron was so sophisticated with numbers and so committed to diversity, he was able to put together the story that I needed to look good. I don't mean that he manipulated the story; I mean that he was able to get the data to show the impact of inclusion, including benchmarking with competitors. He would spend hours, days, studying our competitors to allow us to compare data accurately. I set the goal of being in the top twenty-fifth percentile of our peer group—and when I made it, I had the numbers to back it up."

Erni fulfilled her part of the deal too, first coaching him on those soft skills that he lacked, then giving him the opportunities and exposure that he craved. "We wanted to make sure we were holding our business accountable for getting minority-owned suppliers," she recalled. "I suggested that Aaron cocreate the project, then lead it in partnership with the supplier team. That team really wanted to do it themselves, but I convinced them that he had the financial acumen as well as the diversity and inclusion context. I then sent him, a white guy, to a 'women in finance' conference and a black supplier diversity group. After that he started to organize, host, and speak at supplier conferences at Lehman. I got him the exposure he needed."

Blumenthal spent a few years heading supplier diversity at Lehman, then he asked Erni to fulfill the next part of the deal. "He said he wanted to move to private client work. So I went to George Walker, who was running our private clients team at the time, put in a good word for Aaron, and he got the job. He moved to another bank after Lehman's bankruptcy, asked me for referrals, and started to build a book.

"The deal paid off. He helped me out, then I helped him move on, and he trained his successor."

Making a Deal with a Frenemy

Trevor Phillips's experience with sponsorship began early on, and he has shown special creativity with this powerful tool. One of the many deals he's made took an existing relationship to a new level—turning a man from a possible political opponent into a protégé.

"There's a chap called Simon Woolley," Phillips says, "a little younger than me, and a well-known activist. He's black and he runs a thing called Operation Black Vote or OBV, which started out as a campaign to get out minority voters. But what it has done, and done very successfully and extremely usefully, is train leaders, particularly in politics. At least half a dozen of the ethnically diverse ministers who have been in UK government over the last decade came out of Simon's program. In 1987 there were only four minority MPs. Today I think there are about fifty, and more than half of those people would have come through OBV programs."

Phillips admired many things about Woolley, whom by the early 2000s he'd known for over a decade, but their differences were legion. "He's a good guy, but he and I have never really agreed about politics and race and so on. He would say he's very left wing, and I'm taken by the establishment. However, he had always felt that his radical background shut him out of being heard by the establishment. People would always say we were on the opposite sides of most things."

In 2006, the UK government appointed Phillips chair of a new civil liberties organization, the Equality and Human Rights Commission (EHRC). The EHRC took over the responsibilities that had formerly belonged to three separate commissions, on racial equality, equal opportunities for women, and disability rights. Needless to say, the leaders of these older organizations, who often had strong support inside their communities, were decidedly unhappy about giving up their power and funds to this new commission. Phillips needed an ally, someone who had less of an "establishment" aura and could give him credibility with these different pressure groups.

"I said to Simon, 'Would you be interested in joining?' And he looked at me as if I were mad and said, 'Why would you want me to join? You know I'm going to be a pain in the ass.' And I said, 'That's partly what I want. I need somebody who is going to make things difficult for us. Push back. And there's a deal here. You get to say what you want, but I need you to support the institution. Not be outside throwing rocks. I want you inside making it better. Because I'm creating this thing. I know it's not perfect. But I want to leave things better than I found them.'"

Woolley took Phillips's suggestion, and put himself forward as a candidate for commissioner—but at first he didn't get the spot. The UK government's ministers made appointments to the commission, not Phillips, and one minister in particular wasn't keen on Woolley. So Phillips made his support for Woolley—which was part of the deal—explicit not just to Woolley, but to his many contacts in the government at the time. "I pushed for his appointment," Phillips says, "and I got him appointed."

"What then happened," Phillips continues, "was he joined the commission and he was a pain in the ass. But not from the point of view of saying, 'This organization is useless,' but from the point of view of saying, 'This organization is not doing what it promised. It needs to do better.' And that to me was fine. He was upping our game.

"And it was important to have him on the inside like that, because at that point most of the minority pressure groups, a lot of the women's pressure groups, and all the disability pressure groups wanted to kill the commission. They wanted to kill it, because they had all had their own fiefdoms. And Simon was absolutely vital. He was rock solid in supporting the commission's existence, even as he also pushed for change in it. And that was because we had the deal."

As part of their work on the commission, Phillips and Woolley partnered around a new approach to stop-and-frisk, or stop-and-search, as it's called in the United Kingdom. They developed a new way of collecting and analyzing numbers that proved that the police—even after controlling for other factors, such as income and geography—were far more likely to target blacks than whites. "It got the police forces to change their policy," Phillips says. "I put Simon out as the face of the project, and it got him a lot of credit."

Among the politicians who noticed and supported this initiative was Theresa May, who became prime minister in 2016. "Shortly after her win, she announced, for the first time ever, a race disparity audit," Phillips says. "And when she launched it, who was sitting next to her? Simon Woolley. And that was due to a relationship between them that I coached."

The deal Phillips and Woolley made, in which Phillips got Woolley a seat on the new commission and Woolley provided constructive criticism and credibility with the critics on the left, also included coaching: Phillips giving Woolley advice on how to handle prominent politicians. This paid off big time with Theresa May. But whatever the scorecard between the two men, the truth is this sponsorship deal enabled both men to grow their brand and their reach. And it's not over.

Phillips and Woolley are no longer sponsor and protégé, or even working directly together. But one of the beauties of the sponsor-protégé relationship is how it can evolve into a friendship and an alliance between peers, each with the power and the good will to help out the other. Phillips and Woolley are still a "pain in the ass" for each other now and then, as neither wishes or needs to compromise who they are and what they believe in, but they continue to support each other. "If I need someone to do something, I can ring Simon up, and he'll do it for me," Phillips says.

That's the kind of long-run payoff that sponsorship can bring. However, to reap this benefit and others, sponsors have to invest in specific ways in their protégés—as we'll see in chapter 10.

Breaking It Down

Your sponsorship relationship will truly take off only when your terms are clear. That means explicitly instigating a deal with your potential protégé. When to have this critical conversation can be tricky, and it's not the same for everyone. The tips below can help you decide when the timing is right and how to make the ask.

- **Choose your moment**. If you feel confident that you've found the right person, and you've done your due diligence, you may want to strike the deal quickly, as Tiger Tyagarajan did—but keep inspecting, even after you've committed. If you won't be working shoulder to shoulder, or if you have less experience with sponsorship, you may want to take more time.

- **Factor in the organizational culture**. Another variable here is the organization. In enterprises where sponsorship is well understood, it's easier to instigate a deal quickly—but you still need to continue to vet your pick. In more traditional, less-evolved corporate cultures, where sponsorship may arouse suspicions of favoritism, it's wise to move slowly.

- **Be explicit**. Whether you move fast or slow, whether you use the word "sponsorship" or not, whether you consciously sought out a protégé or the relationship grew organically, there comes a time when you need to make clear to protégés what expectations you have of them, and what they can expect from you.

- **Be open**. Even if you're not yet ready to fully invest in a person (remember how Anne Erni first taught subject matter content, and only then offered opportunities and introductions), you should always be transparent, with your protégé and those around you, about the relationship you're building. Make sure everyone knows that this relationship is about value and that it is a rolling opportunity, open to others too.

10

Invest Three Ways

The economist Lord John Eatwell is currently at the top of his game, president of Queen's College at Cambridge and a peer of the realm. It's hard to believe that in 1970 he was just another postgraduate student, hoping to get a fellowship that might determine whether his university career would gain traction.

Cambridge, like most elite universities (and most *Fortune* 500 companies) is a fiercely competitive place, and for every plum position, there are a ton of people with stellar résumés to fill it. "I'd published papers, I had the qualifications," Eatwell says. "But it was far from certain that I'd get the spot. Academic committees are very political beings. One needs a word in various ears. It just isn't good enough to have the credentials."

The night before the committee was meeting to decide the fellowship, Eatwell had dinner with a sponsor of his, the eminent Italian economist Luigi Pasinetti. By the time dessert rolled around, Pasinetti understood what a critical moment it was for Eatwell.

"He left our dinner, it was past ten at night then, and he walked across Cambridge," Eatwell recalls, "knocking on the doors of members of the committee (who were all close friends of his) to tell them that they had to give the fellowship to me. And they did."

In the years that followed, as Pasinetti expected, Eatwell not only had a brilliant career as an economist. He also kept alive Pasinetti's legacy, the legacy of Pasinetti's sponsor, and the legacy of Pasinetti's sponsor's sponsor, John Maynard Keynes. As Pasinetti hoped and expected, Eatwell, along with one or two other Pasinetti protégés, helped ensure that the Keynesian school of thought survived and thrived into the next generation. Eatwell delivered his side of the bargain.

What Pasinetti did so brilliantly illustrates the next step in the playbook. Ideally, it comes after you've made a deal with a protégé, who for years has been providing performance, loyalty, and a value add. It also usually comes after you've inspired and instructed your protégé, increasing his or her motivation and capacity to deliver for you, your organization, and your field.

The step to take now is to *invest*. You've found a star who deserves to shine. It's time to help them do it. There are three key ways to invest in protégés so that they are more likely to succeed and help you either rise to the top or—if you're already there—embody your brand, trumpet your vision, and deepen your legacy after you step down.

Investment One: Endorse in Noisy Ways

When Jane Shaw retired as chair of Intel's board in 2012, she held a farewell dinner. It was an intimate affair, for her colleagues on the board, a few other very senior people at Intel—and a woman named Rosalind Hudnell.

Who is this woman? the other board members might have murmured to each other. *What is she doing here?* Shaw didn't let the suspense last long. She stood and introduced Hudnell to Intel's leadership, gathered there for dinner. "I want you to know Roz Hudnell," she said, "because the work she is doing is vital to Intel's success." Shaw went on to explain the importance of Hudnell's work as chief diversity officer, work that enabled women and people of color to have a fair shot at success in the company.

"I thought she was a remarkable woman, making great strides for us," Shaw says, explaining why she included Hudnell in the Intel board dinner. "And within the organization, I didn't think she was as valued as she should have been. So when I brought her to that dinner, people paid attention. It led to new opportunities for Roz within the organization. And then she helped me after my retirement establish a network outside of Intel, which has served me so very well." That new network has extended Shaw's influence beyond the scientific and business worlds into a wider world of social engagement, with connections and a higher profile among powerful women leaders from diverse backgrounds.

Shaw's open endorsement of Hudnell is a great illustration of the first way to invest in a protégé. You've instigated a deal and been transparent about it. Now it's time to use your megaphone. Tell not just your immediate colleagues but the world that you're sponsoring this person and why. Endorse their performance, their commitment to the organization, and the added value their experience and skill sets provide. You've tested and developed this person enough to believe in their leadership potential and trustworthiness—let everyone know.

This kind of public endorsement should take place during working hours too. It's one way in which Kerrie Peraino, now leader of people operations for Google's global advisory function, back then a VP at American Express, invested in a then-rising talent, Valerie Grillo.

"I wanted to expose her talent, and I needed to, because the group she was working for at that time was not in the limelight, not center stage at the company," Peraino says. "So I would bring Valerie with me to meetings, where she wouldn't have otherwise been, so that some of my brand and reputation would fall onto her, and people would assume, *If Kerrie's bringing her here, Kerrie must think that she's a significant young talent we should pay attention to.*"

"That was the key moment in my career," Grillo says of that time. "Kerrie provided me the exposure and the opportunity that I needed." Grillo has since risen high in American Express, where she now heads HR for the firm's global consumer business group. That makes her—born and raised in the Bronx in a Puerto Rican family—one of American Express's most senior Latina employees. As such, she's an important inspiration for the firm's women and people of color, a big aid in recruiting others, and part of the legacy that Peraino and others built at Amex.

Unfortunately, CTI's data shows that only 50 percent of male sponsors and 59 percent of female sponsors fully believe in their protégés' leadership potential. On the one hand, skepticism is understandable. Sponsorship is risky. That person may prove to be a poor performer or, even worse, disloyal. And, since so many sponsors instigate a deal quickly—and many of these sponsors haven't the experience that Tiger Tyagarajan or Anne Erni have— they might feel they have not instructed or inspected them thoroughly enough.

On the other hand, the odds of a protégé succeeding rise enormously if his or her sponsor believes in them as well as endorses them. The answer is to move through the steps (instructing, inspecting, and instigating a deal) so that you know that this person deserves your full-throated support—and then you must provide it.

Investment Two: Advocate behind Closed Doors

The second way to invest is to advocate not just in public, but where it really counts: inside the corridors of power. Is a new position opening up? Are pay hikes on the table? What about a rotation that will provide key experience for the next step up? By now, you should be deeply aware of your protégés' strengths—and you should have three protégés, with differentiated skill sets and attributes. So when promotion or other opportunities arise, you are well placed to fill the slot with a protégé who is a great fit.

Put your protégé's name forward and, if necessary, knock on doors as John Eatwell's sponsor did. You can also help your protégés advocate for themselves. When mortgage giant Freddie Mac needed a new chief information officer, its HR chief, Jacqueline Welch, knew just the right person. Welch helped her candidate get the position, then went to work to help her succeed.

"Here at Freddie Mac," Welch explains, "our conservator is very hands-on with respect to the officer corps. This is a $2 trillion balance-sheet organization, but our officer corps is only about 150 people. So it's a small group. When you start bringing in people from the outside, you have to present them a certain way, package them a certain a way, prepare them for questions, and kind of pressure-test them for what they're going to say in response. You also have to figure out who you're going to get support from. I told my candidate, 'Here's how all this plays out at Freddie. These are the things to be mindful of. These are the conversations you have to have. Let's role-play.'"

Prepping your protégé and advocating for them behind closed doors aren't just powerful aids. They're often prerequisites for new talent to get to the top, especially if he or she isn't part of the organization's "old boys' club." But here too, CTI's survey showed, sponsors often fall short. Only 30 percent of men who call themselves sponsors and only 24 percent of women say that they've vigorously advocated for a protégé to get a promotion. That's a big missed opportunity. If you've found a top talent and they've proven their trust worthiness, the higher up they rise, the more they can help you and the organization.

Investment Three: Provide Air Cover

Part of the secret to success is having the freedom to fail now and then. There are unforgivable mistakes—such as disloyalty or dishonesty—and your protégés can't draw on your influence and patience without limit. But there are times when a more junior person needs to know that someone senior has their back in order to take calculated risks. As a sponsor, you can provide air cover to your protégé so that he or she can propose that bold idea or start that pilot project.

That's what IPG's CEO Michael Roth does for his protégé Heide Gardner. "Whenever Heide has said she thinks it would be good if I participated in a meeting that she's running, or if she needs me to send a note or address a group, or she wants me to be visible and support an objective, I do what she asks." To have the CEO at your side when you speak is a pretty powerful statement that he has your back.

And when a protégé's efforts fall short, as everyone's efforts do sometimes, make sure that people in power know that this person deserves a second chance. That's the kind of support that certain people—usually those who have the same personal and educational background as senior management—take for granted. But it's one that many women, people of color, and other previously excluded people lack. Providing air cover is the kind of support that, CTI's survey data shows, only 19 percent of sponsors provide to junior talent.

All these low numbers for sponsors investing in their protégés are, of course, disappointing. But they also show the size of the opportunity. If sponsors are already getting such a boost to their careers from their protégés, just imagine how much more they'd benefit if they invest more substantially in them.

Let's now take a look at sponsors in two different sectors—financial services and consumer goods—who have taken this final step of the sponsorship playbook and done it right, in all three ways, to maximize the benefits to themselves and the organization where they work.

Investing in Hidden Brilliance

"A while back, this guy Farzad comes in for an interview," recalls Mark Hanson, SVP for mortgage securitization and structured finance at Freddie Mac. "We were all completely unimpressed. I went to the colleague who recommended him, and said, 'You talked up Farzad quite a bit but we just didn't see it.' And he said, 'No, no. Go back and talk to him again.' So we did a little digging. He was a Stanford grad who went on to earn a PhD in chemical engineering at Cal Tech. We called the professor that he left as a reference. This professor said, 'Farzad? He's the smartest guy I've seen come through in fifteen years.'

"So we hired him and he did indeed turn out to be the smartest person I've ever worked with. But he's very indirect in how he communicates, so it's hard to see. He's quiet and shy, but now that we see it, we're building entire divisions around him."

It took Hanson a little time to identify Farzad as a protégé, but once he did, he invested in him heavily, not just in resources—you might do that with any talented report—but also by advocating for him and talking him up, in public and behind closed doors.

"There was a time when my boss was a big Wall Street guy," Hanson recalls. "About a year into Farzad's time here this boss said to me, 'I don't get Farzad. All you do is keep talking about him. I've been around him and I don't get him.' Now this boss of mine had all sorts of advice for me on how to develop myself, and I said to him, 'Can I just offer one thing? In your own development program for the next year, can you be more patient and listen to Farzad? And when you don't understand something, ask him again.' He said, 'If you commit to your development goals, I'll do that for you.' Six months later, he knocked on my door, this big Wall Street character, and he said to me, 'Does Farzad know he's the smartest one in this place? He'll never acknowledge it. But I see it now.'"

Hanson also gave Farzad air cover where he needed it most: with the federal government. "Because of his surname, and because he's from Iran, I guess, the authorities thought he was Muslim and he was having a real tough time getting his green card. He would get threatening calls from the immigration office in Baltimore in the middle of the workday and someone would say, 'Get down here now.' This went on for more than five years."

Thanks, in part, to Hanson's support and understanding—providing paperwork to support Farzad's application, and covering for him when he had to talk to or meet with immigration in the middle of a busy workday—Farzad has gotten his green card, as well as the recognition inside Freddie Mac that he deserves. And, of course, Farzad has delivered too, and not just with the standout performance that you'd expect from the smartest guy at Cal Tech.

"A few years back I was offered a big job," Hanson says, "to head up a department at a Wall Street bank. As part of the offer, I was supposed to find five people to take with me. I called Farzad and said, 'There's this opportunity in New York. It would require me to move, but it's big and I need you.' I didn't need to give him any more details than that. He just said, 'If you think it's a good idea, I'm with you. And I can name two or three others we can bring with us.' I didn't end up taking the offer, but I have never forgotten his response to my request. It demonstrated commitment, loyalty, and the degree to which I could rely on him."

Investing outside Your Hierarchy

I've discussed many sponsor-protégé pairs in which sponsors are their protégés' supervisors (or their supervisors' supervisors), but one of the wonderful things about sponsorship is how it can expand your reach beyond the traditional chain of command.

A few years ago, Jonathan Atwood, vice president of communications and sustainable business for Unilever North America, interviewed Mita Mallick for a position as director of communications—effectively, his number two. He didn't offer her the job, since she didn't have quite the right qualifications, but he was so impressed with her that he got her another one.

"I called up the head of HR," he says, "who was looking to create a new position, director of diversity outreach and inclusion and employer brand, and I said, 'Talk to Mita. She's the kind of talent you need. Take a chance on her.'"

The HR head was equally impressed with her and gave her the post. When Mallick reached out to thank Atwood, their relationship—which at this point was simply that of a senior executive recommending a younger one—began to evolve into sponsorship. Atwood's brand of sponsorship, as well as his way of working, depends heavily on inspiring others.

"The personal story, the human story, it's what often gets left behind," he explains. "But it's the most powerful thing. It's what moves people." Atwood has often spoken, inside and outside Unilever, about his own struggles in life, including a battle to overcome alcoholism and stay sober.

"When I met Mita," he says, "I sensed that she had a powerful story to tell. She already knew mine, so I asked her to tell me hers. And she did, and she said afterward it was the first time she'd ever told it to anyone." Her story was one of cultures crossed and barriers overcome. Both of Mallick's grandmothers were child brides, married off at very young ages to small farmers in India. One of her grandfathers was jailed because he was a freedom fighter, fighting for India's independence from British rule. He spent many years behind bars. Her parents came to the United States, where Mallick was born and where she had her own struggles to overcome. Some of her struggles were relatively common—the challenges of coming from a different culture, or of juggling work and motherhood—while others were more specific and personal. Altogether, they are indeed, as Atwood suspected, inspirational.

"I am living proof," Mallick told me, "of what progress can look like in two generations. One of my grandmothers was married off when she was ten years old!"

Atwood realized that if Mallick could find the courage to share her story more broadly, she'd have a powerful tool for winning buy-in for her new role, which involved using diversity to both motivate employees and build Unilever's brand. But the kind of sharing that Atwood suggested can be scary. An ambitious young professional might ask: "Do my bosses, colleagues, and reports really want to hear my personal history? What if they think less of me afterward?"

Atwood understood these risks. So he offered her air cover.

"I said to her, 'I will provide a safe zone. I will have your back if things get a little off track or if people react poorly.' My sponsorship of Mita has had almost nothing to do with the transmission of knowledge," Atwood adds. "At its core, it's been me giving her the space and the support to say her truth."

Mallick succeeded in her new role, and of course storytelling is only one part of it. She also brought her extraordinary marketing skills and expertise in social media to build world-class diversity and inclusion initiatives and link them to the company brand. To offer just one example, as a result of the internal programs and external communications that Mallick helped create and lead, in 2018 Unilever was named the number one company in the United States for working mothers by Working Mother Media.[1]

Meanwhile, Atwood had extended his investment in Mallick to include high-profile speaking opportunities. "Jonathan approached me with a really big speaking opportunity, to be part of a panel at a festival in Bentonville that Walmart sponsors, with several CEOs," Mallick recalls. "At first I said no, I didn't feel up to it. So Jonathan pulled me into his office and said, 'I'm going to help you do this panel because you need to do it—and I'll travel down to give you support.' And he did. And afterward, we were on the phone with our CEO and 180 other top leaders and Jonathan started singing my praises, 'Mita was in Bentonville and she was amazing, she strengthened our relationship with Walmart and built the Unilever brand.'"

His investment in her and advocacy for her have continued, behind closed doors as well as out in the open. "He recently had me go and present to our US board of directors," Mallick says. Naturally, as her sponsor, Atwood didn't let her go in front of the board unprepared.

"He pulled me over the day before the board meeting," Mallick explains, "and he said 'Here's what's going to happen. I'm going to walk you through it. Let's talk about the players in the room and what they feel about this topic. And here are the types of questions that you'll hear.'"

Atwood's imaginative efforts have paid off. Mallick was recently promoted. She's now Unilever North America's head of diversity and cross-cultural marketing. And Atwood has had a big boost too. Even though Mallick has never been Atwood's direct report, his sponsorship of her has brought him big benefits. Her story and her talents have supported him in one of his main tasks at Unilever: using the power of personal purpose to better and more authentically connect employees' motivations with the brand. "Today," he says, "she and I are running a program of personal purpose workshops for every employee at Unilever."

She listens to his ideas, and in part thanks to him, she's in a position to drive them forward. "Too often," Atwood says, "people say they'll do something and they won't. Mita's the exact opposite. She'll come to me three weeks after a conversation to say, 'I was reflecting on something you said then, and this is the action I've taken.'"

And, of course, her success reflects well on him. "She created the D&I platform from scratch," Atwood says. "She created a diversity and inclusion board with Unilever's North American president as the leader and with different functional leaders that meet regularly and have big conversations." Needless to say, all these leaders whom Mallick has brought together know that Atwood is the one who found and cultivated this star.

That's just some of what a protégé can do when you follow the playbook and finally invest full throttle: help you in your own tasks; implement the ideas you don't have time for yourself; and boost your brand in *your* superiors' and colleagues' eyes.

When you've taken those three steps—congratulations! You've finished the playbook and now have a mature sponsor-protégé relationship. But you're not done. On the contrary, you're at the start of a relationship that will keep both of you thriving and rising for many years to come—as the next chapter will show.

Breaking It Down

We've explained how sponsorship helps the sponsor, but in order for your relationship to be truly reciprocal and really pay off, you must invest whole-heartedly in your protégé. They need to understand that you're thoroughly in—and those around you need to see that you support them as star talent. The following tips describe concrete steps you can take to promote, advocate for, and support your protégé.

- **Endorse noisily.** This one's straightforward, though it can take some courage at first. Tell everyone about your protégé. Bring them to meetings. Make introductions. The goal here is not just to be open, but to be boisterous. As I'll explore in chapter twelve, this "noisiness" will also reduce any chance of misunderstandings or malicious gossip.

- **Provide support at a personal level.** Sponsors should not be in the business of "building self-esteem." If a protégé has serious issues on this or any other emotional front, he or she should seek help elsewhere. But the support Atwood lent to Mallick by traveling to Bentonville for her first big speaking event, and the support Hanson lent to Farzad when he struggled with immigration and visa issues, was deeply appreciated and undoubtedly deepened bonds of loyalty.

- **Advocate in the corridors of power** and focus on places and people that your protégé cannot access—or has no leverage with. Shaw was extremely deliberate when she invited Hudnell to attend that Intel board dinner—she knew it would elevate Hudnell's visibility and transform her brand. But diplomacy in high places need not involve fancy dinners, it can be low-key. It might be as subtle as a quiet word in the ear of your boss's boss just before the year-end compensation meeting, to make sure that he or she is fully up to speed on the latest accomplishments of your protégé.

- **Celebrate failure**. The downside of being in your protégé's corner and encouraging him or her to take calculated risks is the possibility of failure. Anticipate this and let your protégé know that if things go wrong, you will help with damage control and advise on remediation. You might even offer to make a phone call or send an email to someone they've disappointed. Obviously you also create limits. As mentioned in a previous chapter, "three strikes and you're out" is a reasonable rule of thumb.

11

Integrate and Bring
It All Together

Do the seven steps I've described in this playbook seem like a lot?
On the one hand, they *are* a lot. On the other hand, your protégé
should be doing most of the work along the way—whether it's seeking
you out for instruction or delivering the performance that takes a load
off your shoulders and helps propel both of you up the ladder.

Sponsor-protégé relationships build on each other and transform
not just your career, but the organization where you work. They can
grow and cascade over time and across divisions, transforming not
just careers, but an entire organization.

I've had the good fortune to work with many successful sponsors at many forward-looking companies. Indeed, with support and
assistance from my colleagues at CTI, I've helped put sponsorship
programs in place in more than thirty companies. Most of these organizations and their leaders—as well as many others that I've only

observed—could serve as models. But since EY was gracious enough to grant me multiple one-on-one interviews with half a dozen senior leaders involved in sponsorship and sponsorship initiatives, it's the EY story that I'll explore here.

The story starts with Steve Howe, the recently retired US chairman and managing partner and EY Americas managing partner. His approach to sponsorship has created a cascade of powerful, reciprocal relationships—first with his protégés, and then through his protégés' protégés—that has benefited EY across the decades and around the world, even extending to an unprecedented new initiative in China.

He began his sponsorship with a classic case: a bond between two ambitious and talented men who were working together. In 1987, Howe was in the middle ranks of Ernst & Young LLP (EY US), working on an important account, with a major Wall Street bank. A young accountant named Ken Marshall joined his team, and though Howe was Marshall's supervisor, the two men were quickly working shoulder to shoulder on arcane tasks that required a different set of accounting skills than usual. Howe and Marshall developed a strong enough partnership that they decided to challenge the status quo: they wanted to rewrite the software that EY US used to support this complex audit of an important client.

"We got shouted out of the leadership team's office," Marshall recalls. "We were told we didn't really understand software and were in over our heads, but we went off and redesigned our software by ourselves anyway. I think that was where Steve realized that I was capable of getting things done and not afraid to face up to authority." By their third audit together, the two had succeeded in making process improvements that made audits more efficient and effective.

That experience was what enabled Howe to identify Marshall as a talent worthy of his special investment. "It became clear to me that Ken was a tremendous asset," Howe says. "I realized I had to give him opportunities, leverage him, and get him in front of more people. I also needed to surround myself with more people like him."

Inspiration, Instruction, and Investment

In 1997, at about the time that Marshall was promoted to partner, EY US lost the account that he and Howe were working on after the client merged with another firm. "We were all very invested in that account," Marshall confides. "I almost actually left the firm at that point but Steve got me righted—and moving in a different direction." Marshall also learned simply by watching Howe. "Steve didn't sit around brooding, licking his wounds over this," Marshall recalls. "There was a lot of leadership by example."

Though Howe was no longer Marshall's supervisor, he still kept an eye on him. From time to time he would let him know about opportunities and offer advice. When, for example, Marshall was asked to lead the International Financial Reporting Standards (IFRS Markets) team and later the Financial Accounting Advisory Services (FAAS) practice, he found that he was stretched beyond his comfort zone. In particular he had trouble interacting with a broader swath of the organization. Forging political relationships in order to push through bureaucracy frustrated him.

"I would say, 'Ken, these people are doing their job too,'" Howe says. "'You need to engage with them.' I knew Ken had had a mentor who was an impressive rainmaker, who would have given him the advice of 'don't worry about the administrators, at the end of the day if you're making rain then you will be fine.' I had to coach Ken to a more rounded and balanced place. I said, 'Ken, that's why this other rainmaker only went so far. You can go farther if everyone is included and respected.'"

"There were certainly times when my administrative skills were not my strong suit," Marshall concedes. Though he notes that when Howe admonished him, it was always behind closed doors and with advice on how to go forward. "In the course of your career, you're going to slip up," Marshall adds. "When you do, being able to acknowledge that to someone, saying 'Hey, I messed up,' and knowing that person is going to help is so vital."

A little later when EY was sending people to work in Switzerland, Howe advised Marshall to seize the opportunity and Marshall ended up spending three and a half years in Zurich. "It was an amazing growth experience and great for my résumé," he says. "Without Steve looking out for me I would never have found or gotten that position."

Marshall showed his gratitude to his sponsor in two ways. "In Europe Ken performed at an extraordinary level and this produced reflected glory," Howe says. Marshall also put Howe in front of important European clients and was careful to talk up his leader's accomplishments in advance of these meetings. Looking back on this period Howe says, "He made me look good at every turn."

The relationship between Howe and Marshall evolved as both men became more senior. Marshall sees his value to his sponsor as taking a different turn. His biggest role in recent years has been providing honest feedback. "Since I've been responsible for this practice in many marketplaces—and they range from Canada to South America—I'm in the trenches and hear a lot from people on what they think about the way the business is being run. When I report back to Steve he finds my unvarnished feedback very helpful."

Including Diverse Perspectives

Inclusion has long been a keystone of Howe's approach to sponsorship. It has helped him build alliances that extend his reach beyond the classic case—of two men with complementary skill sets—that he so successfully forged with Marshall. In the late 1990s, for instance, after several female senior managers at EY approached him to express frustration about their prospects at the organization, particularly after maternity leaves when they had new parenting responsibilities, Howe saw an opportunity. He pushed hard to shift the organization's perspective. In part thanks to his efforts, women began to get promoted while also maintaining a balance with family—thus creating an abiding loyalty among women in the organization.

This allegiance turned into a major asset, as the increasingly impressive number of female executives in the leadership ranks of EY became role models and advocates for a younger generation of dynamic high-achieving women. Sponsorship, in its forthrightness and transparency, brought women's ambitions and advancement out of the shadows, emboldening them to seek opportunities without apology or equivocation. It was also a boost for the men who sponsor them. "Yes, some might just sit on the sidelines and say, 'This is just too risky,'" says Karyn Twaronite, the EY global diversity and inclusiveness officer, referring to male executives considering sponsoring female employees. "But if you don't sponsor them, you won't be shaping future leaders for the betterment of the firm."

The message about the power of inclusion has spread throughout the organization. "We have smart, amazing and talented clients, and they lead organizations with really complex problems to solve," continues Twaronite. "It is not possible to provide client service at the level they need without diverse and inclusive teams around. The best and the brightest ideas don't come from the same place any longer. It's just not possible anymore."

Extending Your Reach—and Encouraging a Protégé's Growth

Steve Howe met Kate Barton in 2006, when she moved to New York City to run the firm's Northeast tax practice. They chatted at events and occasionally their work intersected. She had "raw material," Howe recalls. "She was very bright, hardworking, a get-things-done kind of person. But I also saw she might need some help thinking about how to build relationships. Sometimes if you're doing great work, you think that things will just happen, others will recognize it naturally. I felt I could guide her in that respect, help her to become more of a stand-out, to put herself squarely in the line of sight of leadership."

One afternoon, Howe called Barton and asked her to come to his office. He confided in her that she was being considered for the EY Americas vice chair of tax—a position that would put her on the EY US Executive Committee. Although Howe said he didn't know if it would happen for her this time around, he felt it would be worth it for her to make her best effort. "Steve said he had a lot of faith and confidence in me," Barton recalls, "and that, if this didn't work, there could be future roles where I would get on the Executive Committee."

As it turned out, Barton didn't get the job, but eleven months later, Howe called Barton again. "I want to let you know that the firm is asking the incumbent [EY Americas vice chair of tax] to move to Europe and take a significant global role," Howe explained, "so the position is open again." Barton was in the mix once more. At Howe's urging, she put together a PowerPoint presentation for the executive committee describing what she'd accomplished at EY and what she would do if she were appointed the EY Americas vice chair of tax.

This time, in large part thanks to the presentation that Howe had advised her to make—and which set her apart from the other candi-dates—Barton got the job.

From there, Barton and Howe developed a mutually beneficial sponsorship relationship. Sometimes, as with Marshall, Howe coached Barton on her interpersonal politics, advising her to slow down and collaborate, bringing everyone on a project along with her, rather than barreling ahead on her own. Sometimes, Barton stopped by Howe's office just to make him laugh. Sometimes, Howe explains, the two got on the phone to fine-tune the agenda for a meeting, speaking in a kind of shorthand they've developed over the years. "It will just be: 'There are three business issues,'" says Howe, "'and in addition I'm really frustrated with X.'"

Since Barton, Marshall, and other Howe protégés have now become extraordinary successes in their own right, Howe has a reputation for being able to spot talent early on. And, in turn, Barton and Marshall are on the lookout for untapped potential among those that might otherwise go unseen.

One of the protégés that Barton, inspired by Howe, took on, has opened up a big new market for the firm.

Investing in Skill Gaps—and Building a New Market

Barton first met Shau Zhang when Zhang was just a manager in EY's Boston office. There Barton saw her knock a presentation out the park and win a client for the firm. It was all the more impressive because Zhang, back then, had heavily accented English and presentation skills that needed some work.

Barton took her aside to learn something more about this impressive employee. As Zhang remembers that early conversation: "I told her how I came to the United States in my early twenties with just $200 in my pocket, speaking hardly any English. Somehow I made my way through college, into an entry-level position at EY, and now I supported a variety of clients and led as well as delivered on several projects. I told her I even occasionally joined Bostonians for Red Sox games! My message to her was, 'Everything's possible. Nothing's impossible.'"

Excited by having found what she thought might be a standout talent, Barton decided to invest in Zhang. She quickly saw that Zhang didn't need inspiration. She had that already. As Zhang recalls it, "You just walk the hallway in front of the tax partners' windowed offices and you see a lack of diversity. You don't see a woman let along a woman of color. You just don't. So I told Kate, 'I want to be the first female minority who actually comes from mainland China to make partner at the firm.' Kate's response was immediate, 'Shau, let's do it.'"

Barton focused her efforts on closing Zhang's skills gaps and persuaded the firm to underwrite the cost of one-on-one English language classes. This was out of the ordinary. EY did indeed provide language training, but at Zhang's level group classes were the norm. Barton also provided some presentation training. "I always had excellent content, but I didn't have the confidence that comes with superior language skills," says Zhang. "I also needed to learn to present and to deal with questions. Normally, in a Chinese school, communication is one-way, the teacher gives a lecture and students almost never raise a hand or ask a question. Pushback isn't stressed at all. But how are you going to convince others if you're not thoroughly convinced yourself? I practiced looking people in the eye and engaging in discussion and debate."

In providing instruction for Zhang, Barton was modeling herself after Howe and setting her protégé up for success. "The last thing I want is to have Shau fail," Barton says. "A big part of my success is that when I give a young talent I'm sponsoring a big opportunity, I'm also going to give them resources to make sure they succeed." Practical support builds confidence and trust and deepens the two-way dialogue between sponsor and protégé, allowing the relationship to become more of a partnership.

As Zhang proved herself, Barton upped her investment, publicly praising her and advocating behind closed doors—including with her own sponsor, Steve Howe, to whom she introduced Zhang.

One of Howe's immediate—and favorable—impressions of Zhang was that she knew how to be proactive and do the lion's share of driving the sponsor-protégé relationship. "Sometimes the sponsor doesn't have the time," Howe says, "But she (Zhang) went into this saying 'Steve, I need you on this. Kate I need you on that.' She's asked me for help in building stronger relationships with some of our senior leaders. And she's asked me for help adding resources to the business; bringing in more people from outside, bilingual people; and watching out for (and when appropriate, putting in an encouraging word for) key players up for promotion to senior manager or partner. She realizes that it's a two-way street and she's going to engage with it and make good use of it."

Barton was ready to commit to her protégé wholeheartedly: "When EY was ready to set up its China Overseas Investment Network (COIN) to provide services to Chinese companies doing business in the United States," Barton says, "I realized Zhang had the prowess to lead the practice. We needed her stellar track record in the tax practice, her cross-cultural skill sets (her ability, for example, to speak three languages, Chinese, Russian, and English), and her entrepreneurial flair." "We need everything you can bring to the table," Zhang recalls Barton saying to her. "You are the one."

Even at this celebratory moment Barton found herself giving Zhang some unvarnished feedback, echoing advice Howe had once given her. Barton counseled Zhang on how to moderate her self-described "go-go-go" personality once she was in charge of a bigger team. "She's wonderfully aggressive," Barton says, "But sometimes an aggressive woman can be misunderstood, or there are times when someone could take special offense because of cultural differences. I worked with her to be more artful in her assertiveness."

Zhang still leads COIN today. Over the last eight years she has built the practice from the ground up, making it into a $100 million business. "And it's growing rapidly. That is so important to our firm," says Howe. "We need to create dynamism between the United States and China. It's a real legacy play."

But there's another legacy play taking place here too: it is strikingly rare for a woman to bring another woman forward in business no matter how talented. And Barton took on a woman who was also ethnically and culturally different. Had Barton not sponsored this remarkable woman she might never have fulfilled her enormous potential and EY would have missed out on a great deal of value.

Establishing Organizational Sponsorship Programs

Throughout this book, I have focused on how individuals can use sponsorship to advance their own careers and make their organizations more successful. But it's worth calling out that some organizations have put in place formal sponsorship programs, which individuals can take advantage of—especially to cross lines of gender, race, and geography to become more inclusive in their sponsorship.

EY US has an inclusive leadership program that brings high-performing female and ethnically diverse partners in contact with senior partners and executive coaches. It doesn't automatically lead to a sponsor-protégé relationship. That decision always must lie with the sponsor, who will have to identify on his or her own if a prospect is worth significant investment. But these programs can kick-start a relationship and support initial development efforts.

In the EY US program, "you have women and ethnically diverse partners that are 'pre-cleared,'" Twaronite says. "They're proven leaders who get assigned an executive board member as a mentor. Some visit clients together, and some break bread and have dinner. It becomes no different than if they'd met on the golf course with clients, which typically many more male colleagues have had more opportunities to do."

By the time CTI published its first study on sponsorship in 2010, Howe had long been striving for more inclusive leadership. Working with CTI and adding practical insight to several new CTI research studies on the sponsor effect, EY US was able to give new language and meaning to its efforts in this area, validating what Howe had long understood intuitively: that sponsorship is good for business, and has a positive and quantifiable impact on the bottom line. As a consequence EY US has deepened its commitment to sponsorship, weaving it into its talent processes and compensation structures. Now, when leaders proactively develop young talent that is rich in diversity—crossing lines of experience and discipline as well as gender, race, and geography—this is factored into promotions and bonuses.

Howe didn't need this kind of structure to find diverse talent to sponsor, but he hasn't hesitated to take advantage of it. Over the years, he's worked with about two dozen women and minorities through the EY US inclusive leadership program. "At a minimum," he says, "it's mentoring, and some of these turn into sponsoring relationships." Among the few whom he not only mentored but also identified as protégé is a woman named Kelly Grier.

On July 1, 2018, fifteen years after the program first assigned Grier to Howe, she succeeded him as the US chair and managing partner and EY Americas managing partner. As we'll see in this book's last chapter, a common use of sponsorship—one that external research indicates is favorable for an enterprise's performance—is grooming a successor for the top slot.

The Payoffs for EY

It's been a long journey for Steve Howe and his protégés, but the payoffs for the organization have been manifold. When just a middle manager, Howe found a brilliant rookie accountant, Ken Marshall. The two first revamped the audit process for a major client, then Howe kept this star talent from leaving the firm at a challenging moment. The two continued to support each other as Howe became CEO and Marshall became head of a major division. Other protégés of Howe's took on other leading roles, and by including and fostering diverse talent, Howe's sponsorship has helped make the organization an employer of choice for women. This inclusive approach also opened up a new and fast-growing market for the firm in China. Finally, sponsorship enabled Howe to have the perfect person in place when it came time for the board to choose his successor.

It's a huge credit to sponsorship's power that it can deliver on so many fronts and can last even beyond a leader's tenure at the firm. But there are also new risks to this relationship in this era of #MeToo, although it is possible to navigate them, as we'll see in the next section.

Part Three

———————•———————

DANGERS AND LEGACIES

12

#MeToo and the
Third Rail

Sexual misconduct is the "third rail" for sponsor-protégé relation-ships: no one can touch it and emerge unscathed. But just as with a real third rail, no one will force you to go there, and some simple precautions can keep everyone out of harm's way. The fear of sexual misconduct and its accompanying dangers isn't a reason to avoid spon-sorship; it's a reason to do it right.

I hesitate to call the awareness of sexual harassment at work new, because many women and men have long been aware that a distress-ing number of men in senior positions will use their power to extract sexual favors. Sometimes they use physical force. Sometimes they offer benefits at work or threaten retaliation. When they've had what they want, they use that same power to cover up their misconduct, thus avoiding consequences for themselves. Their victims almost always suffer both psychologically and professionally.

These exploitative behaviors are as old as the hills, but with 2017 came new media attention and perhaps a new public attitude. That was the year the #MeToo movement began, when a wave of women (and some men) came forward, in a chorus of pain, to denounce the predatory sexual behavior of certain men in power.

CTI data shows that the horror stories appearing regularly in the press aren't isolated cases. A CTI study published in July 2018 found that, among white-collar workers, 34 percent of women have experienced sexual harassment from a colleague, and 7 percent have experienced sexual assault.[1] Some industries are worse than others, as figure 12-1 illustrates, with nearly 41 percent of women in media reporting harassment, but even in the straitlaced legal world, 22 percent of women report harassment.[2]

FIGURE 12-1 WOMEN WHO HAVE EXPERIENCED
SEXUAL HARASSMENT FROM A COLLEAGUE

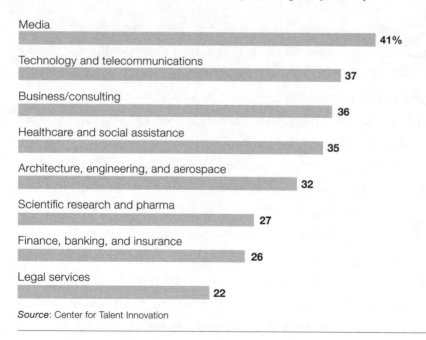

Women who have been sexually harassed by a colleague, by industry:

Media — 41%
Technology and telecommunications — 37
Business/consulting — 36
Healthcare and social assistance — 35
Architecture, engineering, and aerospace — 32
Scientific research and pharma — 27
Finance, banking, and insurance — 26
Legal services — 22

Source: Center for Talent Innovation

The danger extends to women across the board. CTI data shows that 37 percent of white and Latina women report having suffered harassment, as do 25 percent of black women and 23 percent of Asian women.[3]

The damage from such behavior affects not just individuals but also the enterprises where they work. The hit to share prices and company valuations can easily cost millions of dollars, according to a 2018 study in the *Journal of Financial Economics*, and expensive class-action lawsuits and fraud investigations often deepen the drain of value.[4]

Consider Nike, where women reported systemic harassment and discrimination, which it now appears didn't just cripple these women's careers. It also likely led to a dearth of women in leadership, which in turn helped cause Nike's relative lack of success in the fast-growing women's athletic market. When in 2018 the evidence of misbehavior became too strong for leadership to ignore, Nike's CEO Mark Parker eased out eleven senior male executives, including the brand president.[5] This exodus put downward pressure on share price.

Men too can be victims of sexual misconduct. In CTI's study, 13 percent of men reported sexual harassment from a colleague. Five percent reported assault. Black men are particularly likely to face such crimes, with 21 percent reporting harassment and 7 percent reporting sexual assault. Of the men who have suffered harassment from a colleague, more than half (57 percent), have been harassed by another man.

Consensual Sex Is a Danger Too

Even if a sexual relationship between an executive or manager and a more junior employee is consensual, it's still almost certain to erode trust and value cause great damage. The damage begins with the couple involved, especially the junior partner, who is usually a woman. It extends to their colleagues, subordinates, and everyone who works on their teams.

The 2018 CTI survey asked employees what they thought about sleeping with the boss and found that it is a) common and b) roundly condemned. Eleven percent of employees said that they knew of someone on their team who had a sexual relationship with a boss or supervisor. Seventy-one percent of these employees said that they found the relationship inappropriate.

The reasons for this disapproval aren't ideological; they're pragmatic. Here's why:

- *Morale takes a hit.* Twenty-five percent reported a falloff in morale on the team when a boss or supervisor was sleeping with a subordinate.

- *They lose respect.* Twenty-two percent said the team lost respect for the boss or supervisor involved, and another 17 percent said the team lost respect for the boss's lover.

- *Performance and productivity suffer.* Fourteen percent reported that team performance deteriorated when the boss was sleeping with a subordinate, and 11 percent reported that team productivity declined.

In some of the follow-up interviews we held after fielding this survey, respondents gave us more detail about the problems that manager-subordinate affairs caused, including a distorted workplace environment for everybody.

If you think someone is having an affair with the boss, you have to treat her with kid gloves. Otherwise she might bad-mouth you to her lover. And you certainly can't do anything but praise her to the boss, for fear that he'll be angry or defensive. He is sleeping with her after all! Such suspicions and resentments feed into the work dynamics of the team and performance slumps.

So there you have it. If you want a demoralized, mistrustful, unproductive, and uncommunicative team, an affair with a protégé—or any subordinate—will give you all that in a hurry.

Don't Let Fears Stop Sponsorship

Beyond the misconduct itself, professional women across the board suffer an additional burden: men fearful of suspicions or malicious gossip will avoid taking them on as protégés. The CTI survey revealed that about 40 percent of men and women (with no significant difference between the genders) agree with the statement that "recent publicity about sexual harassment at work makes it even less likely that a male leader will sponsor a female protégé—even if she deserves it."[6]

Stories of this unfortunate behavior abound. An orthopedic surgeon with a practice outside Chicago told the *New York Times* that he now avoids being alone with female colleagues and especially with subordinates. "I'm very cautious about it because my livelihood is on the line," he said. "If someone in your hospital says you had inappropriate contact with this woman, you get suspended for an investigation, and your life is over. Does that ever leave you?"[7]

The same article quoted an anonymous venture capitalist saying that many men in his field are now avoiding one-on-one meetings with women entrepreneurs and potential hires. "Before, you might have said, 'Of course I would do that, and I will especially do it for minorities, including women in Silicon Valley,'" the investor said. "Now you cancel it because you have huge reputational risk all of a sudden."[8]

But is sponsorship across lines of gender really too dangerous to touch in the era of #MeToo? The answer is no—it must not be, since overcoming this kind of mistrust is a business imperative. As the leaders of EY and many, many other companies know, gender diversity in leadership is a competitive strength. A report by CTI, *Innovation, Diversity, and Market Growth,* showed that when teams have at least one member that reflects the gender of their end user, the *entire team* is more than twice as likely (61 percent versus 25 percent) to report that they understand the targeted marketplace.[9] For wealth and asset management, the power of women leaders to help their organizations tap a $5.1 trillion market in the United States alone—assets managed solely by women—was the subject of a CTI book, *Harness the Power of the Purse.*[10] If you're not sponsoring top female talent in your company, odds are good that they'll go somewhere else where their chances to thrive are better, and you'll lose the benefits of having their "gender-smart" perspectives.

Fortunately, it is possible—and necessary—to build sponsorship relationships in a way that drastically reduces the risk of sexual misconduct or malicious gossip. It's possible for men and women to interact in the workplace with trust and professionalism.

How to Sponsor Safely in the Era of #MeToo

Surely the readers of this book are well-intentioned men and women, eager to boost their careers, their organizations, and the younger talent that surrounds them through sponsorship; but what might hold back these well-intentioned individuals is a sense of mounting risk and a fear of misunderstandings and gossip.

The answer to those fears is an atmosphere of openness and respect. To foster that atmosphere, both sponsors themselves and the organizations where they work can take some concrete steps.

Here's what individual sponsors can do.

- *Be noisy.* Make sure everyone in your orbit knows whom you're sponsoring and why. As Kerrie Peraino puts it, "Men should be boisterous in their sponsorship of female talent. Meet with her where everybody can see. When you bring her to a meeting and ask her to do a presentation, talk about it in the context of her development and your working together." Trevor Phillips echoes this advice: "It's too easy for people to put other narratives on what you're doing if you haven't. Send a memo outlining why you are sponsoring this remarkable talent. Tell people in meetings. Be absolutely clear."

- *Be public.* You don't need to stay up late drinking in a bar to build a bond. Meet with your protégé in the company cafeteria, in the Starbucks around the corner, or in your office with the door open. "We have nice cafeterias," Mark Hansen from Freddie Mac says, "That's where I meet. It's easier to understand where a protégé is coming from, or what their professional aspirations are, in a place less formal than an office. And phones are not ringing. Breakfast, lunch, even just a coffee. It's all good."

- *Share but don't overshare.* You can't build a bond without self-revelation. But don't go overboard and share things that cause discomfort or misunderstanding. Show just a little of that soft underbelly that we all have. Kevin Lord had perfect pitch. He told Marsheila Hayes his hopes and fears for his children as they applied to college and went out for their first jobs. Hayes was a recent graduate and eager to be helpful. She ended up providing advice and practical guidance. Once he'd started this conversation, it was easy for her to ask his help with her graduate school applications, and the two of them started to build a deeper professional relationship.

- *Consider family activities.* As the relationship deepens, consider introducing your protégé to your family. Have your protégés over on Sunday for brunch with your spouse or partner. If you and your protégés have children, bring them all to a zoo or museum on a weekend. Family activities are a great way to deepen bonds while allaying suspicions, rather than creating them. George W. Bush and Condoleezza Rice bonded over workouts in the gym and summer visits to his family. Bush finally came to view her "like a sister."[11]

- *Show respect and do not patronize.* It's not hard for a protégé—especially a young female protégé—to catch a vibe of condescension. "Are you at the meeting to dial into the conference call and fetch coffee, or are you there to contribute your smarts and your experience?" Think of how Kent Gardiner showed his awareness of Sonia's significant capabilities from the get-go, and gave her his full attention as he worked with her to identify the special area in which she could excel. He then put her in front of clients, demonstrating to his colleagues his confidence in her.

- *Remember the risks of exclusion.* Excluding high-performing women from advancement doesn't just limit the organization; it can get a male boss in trouble too. It takes multiple incidents to reach the legal bar for "sexual harassment"—but only one act of exclusion from a deserved career opportunity to qualify for sex-based discrimination.

- *For senior leaders: set a tone from the top.* If you're in a position where others in the organization will follow your example, set one: publicly reaffirm your commitment to sponsoring talented protégés of the opposite sex.

Individuals have to do most of the work, since sponsorship is fundamentally a bond and an investment between two individuals. But organizations can and should act to support and enable sponsor-protégé relationships across the divides of gender. This is good for the bottom line and will foster more balanced and respect-filled leadership cultures. Here are a few measures that can help create a corporate culture where fear of harassment is rare, because misconduct is rare:

- *Establish zero tolerance for sexual misconduct.* Install explicit company policies so victims and bystanders feel empowered to speak up, and so predators know that punishment awaits. For example, forbid nondisclosure agreements over settlements in sexual misconduct cases. NDAs were a big reason why serial predators such as Harvey Weinstein could keep abusing women for so many years.

- *Update training and education.* Fresh insights into the culture of toxic masculinity, the role of bystanders, and the potential for male allyship have opened up new possibilities to teach employees how to engage respectfully across gender lines, and how to support victims and push back against perpetrators.

- *Create new channels for reporting and remediation.* To reduce the often-justified fear of suffering reprisals for reporting misconduct, create special channels that allow employees to bypass managers and HR. Technological tools such as information escrows and the AllVoices app are examples.[12]

- *Highlight common values.* Remind employees, executives, and junior staffers alike that they're on the same side. A workplace culture free from bad behavior benefits the organization and everyone in the organization. (Except for predators, who should not be welcome inside it.) The vast majority of women and men want sponsor-protégé relationships to be free from sexual aggression.

With these few simple rules, sponsoring a younger person of another gender (or the same gender, for members of the LGBTQ community) won't constitute a reputational risk. Instead, its transformative power will boost the productivity and careers of both sponsor and protégé, support diversity in top management, and foster a healthier work environment for men and women throughout the organization.

13

Legacy

At some point, we all move on from our current professional roles. Maybe we take a new job in a different organization. Maybe we switch careers. And sooner or later, all our professional lives come to an end.

But many ambitious professionals would like to leave a positive mark behind: a new culture of innovation; a new market or a return to profitability; greater diversity and sustainability; or simply the knowledge of a job well done, and the confidence that you've handed off the baton to someone who will keep your good work from going to waste.

This ambition applies at every level of an organization. You don't have to be at the very top to want to feel—with reason—that you've left the organization better than how you found it.

Sponsorship is one of the best ways to create that kind of legacy. After all, in most organizations, your successor can undo your work; but if that successor is a protégé, whom you've identified as a loyal, value-adding high performer, and then inspired, instructed, and inspected until you're finally ready to instigate a deal and really invest in them, the odds are good that they'll not just carry on your legacy but grow it.

CTI data quite clearly shows that there's a "legacy effect" for leaders at every level of the organization. Among our survey respondents, who ranged from entry-level professionals to C-suite executives, 39 percent of those with a protégé deemed themselves "satisfied with their professional legacies." Only 25 percent of those who don't have protégés said the same.

From Sponsorship to Succession

This notion of a legacy brings the discussion back to Steve Howe, who used sponsorship to create a cascade of benefits. One was supporting his own rapid progression in EY US. Another was developing a bench of talent, rich in diversity, which boosted the organization's success in the marketplace and helped make it an employer of choice for women and people of color. I call Howe's success with sponsorship a cascade, since he not only identified, instructed, and invested in protégés over the years, but these protégés have had their own protégés. They in turn are driving outstanding results for EY US, including a successful new line of business in China.

These accomplishments already add up to quite a legacy for Howe. To add to that, he recently saw a protégé succeed him as US chairman and managing partner and EY US managing partner. You don't have to be a CEO to care about who follows in your footsteps, but his example is worth emulating, no matter where you are in your career: it reveals a number of careful steps, slowly building up to a full investment over many years. Because when you're grooming a protégé to succeed you and carry your baton, you'll need some extra intentionality.

Starting Slowly and Standing Back

Howe met Kelly Grier through EY's inclusive leadership program, which I described in chapter 11. By that time, she was already a successful partner and a proven performer, and his first personal impression was that she was "smart, energetic, strategic, thoughtful, and very proactive." They proceeded to meet three or four times a year, usually for about two hours.

"He would give me latitude just to speak openly, to ask questions, talk about what I didn't know," Grier recalls. "He was never prescriptive in his advice."

"It was clear to me that Kelly Grier could do great things," Howe says. "I wanted to help build her experiences and demonstrate her capabilities to others." And so he began to subtly guide Grier in their conversations—offering stories from his own life, and presenting a broader vantage point on her career and on the organization.

Howe also understood that at times the best thing a sponsor can do is stand back and watch—and that watching includes inspection. "Somebody can have all of the right attributes but when they are tested, you see a different person emerge," he says. "An emerging talent can be strategic and thoughtful, but as someone steps into bigger and bigger roles, the unexpected occurs."

Upping the Investment

Grier more than met the challenge, so Howe encouraged her to put her hat in the ring for the global advisory council and Americas advisory council—two groups of elected partners who meet with the chairman (Howe was the chairman of the Americas advisory council) on a quarterly basis. "It's a great experience, to interact with both the partners and the management team," Howe says. "I knew it would lift her visibility." Grier won the spot, and the council liked her performance so much that its members next elected her to be their presiding partner.

Howe's next advice for Grier was unexpected: for her to consider serving as EY Americas vice chair of talent. "I was very surprised," Grier says. "That was a hard turn, not a slight turn, from the path that I was on, which had been all about the markets."

But Howe was thinking ahead, as a good sponsor does. Once protégés have proven exceptional qualities—and by this stage Grier had—it's time to position them for leadership and the organization.

For the organization, Howe wanted someone who could connect the markets, the business, and the talent agenda, as Grier could. For Grier, he wanted additional exposure and experience.

"We're 75,000 people in the Americas and 260,000 people around the world," he says. "We need to recruit the best, develop the best, and make sure that they have the best opportunities. So for Kelly to emerge as the candidate for the top talent—and there were several very prominent senior partners on that list—was a major achievement. And, having gotten to know her, I was able to contribute to the board seeing her as the strong option."

"He explained that it was a role that would bring me onto the [executive] board," Grier says of the position, "and that the exposure I would have to the business of our firm, and to the leaders of it, would be invaluable." Grier won the position and here too, Howe observed as Grier went on to excel at her new job.

"I saw Kelly apply smarts, intellect, relationship skills, and strategic thinking," he says. "I also saw a toughness in her that our business leaders need." That toughness had first appeared on the global advisory council, where she represented the partners in negotiations, but as vice chair of talent she had to not just invest, but also disinvest from parts of the organization.

Prepping Her for the Top Spot

A year after Grier became EY's talent leader for the Americas, she and Howe sat down again to talk about her future. "I hadn't been in that role very long," she says. "A year is a really short tenure for the vice chair of talent. But the opportunity arose to fill a couple of other roles that were also board roles. Steve asked me: Did I want to potentially return to Chicago as vice chair and central region managing partner, stay the course in the talent role, or try for the markets vice chair role?

"Steve had told me early on in my career that he saw my range of capabilities as very broad. As talent leader, I'd created a talent agenda strategy and supported its execution. Before the talent role, in the central region, as a market segment leader and office managing partner, I'd focused on really making a market for the firm and demonstrating market leadership.

"The role as vice-chair and central region managing partner would bring all that together. For that, you have to be a holistic leader. You have full responsibility. You own the market, you own the people, and you own everything in between. If I took it, for the first time in my career I'd have full P&L responsibilities.

"We talked very openly about it. We talked through the various scenarios and the options, and I later learned that Steve had a strong point of view as to which of those paths I should take, but he never gave me instructions. It was much more of a rich and informed conversation that we had that naturally evolved my thinking to ultimately take the central region vice chair role."

Not by coincidence, this new role for Grier, with its multiple responsibilities that in many ways mirror what the head of the firm must do, set up Grier for what would prove to be her next position: at the top. A versatile leader himself, as the CEO of such a large organization must be, Howe had been looking to develop similar flexibility in Grier.

Transitioning to New Leadership

"My last and, some might say, most important job in leading the firm was to conduct a process that was fair and thorough to identify my successor, to have that process lead to the right candidate, and then to devote myself to the transition," Howe says. "Kelly won out and for the first time, EY Americas and EY US will have a woman at the helm, but Kelly is not there because she is a woman. She is there because she is the best candidate. And that's a great statement about the organization."

"Steve has been just so completely present in the most formative stages of my journey as a leader," Grier says. "Every step along the way, Steve has been there with me, even more than I understood at the time."

After the partners voted in late 2017 for Grier to succeed Howe as US chairman and managing partner and EY Americas managing partner, Howe took Grier aside and walked her through their fifteen-year relationship. Grier heard his praise with great pleasure, but she also heard a message. "I didn't get here by coincidence," she says. "My journey had a great deal of intentional effort on Steve's part behind it. He took a lot of deliberate actions over many, many years that were incredibly significant. And this is the mark of a great leader. There is no greater responsibility that a CEO has than to secure the future by investing in and growing a successor."

A study by Spencer Stuart demonstrates just how wise it is for a CEO to groom a protégé as a successor, as figure 13-1 illustrates.[1] The Spencer Stuart data shows that internal hires as CEOs do better than external ones. If the company is in good shape (as judged by performance relative to industry peers) when a new CEO steps in, 43 percent of outsiders perform poorly, compared to 31 percent of insiders, Spencer Stuart calculates. In companies coming off subpar performance, 48 percent of externally hired CEOs perform poorly, compared to 34 percent of internal hires.

In addition, an internal hire, the Spencer Stuart survey shows, doesn't mean someone you just brought in a year or two ago. It means someone the current CEO has been grooming for years. In fact, what Spencer Stuart calls "insider-outsiders" (CEOs appointed after eighteen months or less inside the company) are the worst bets of all, with 47 percent performing poorly.[2]

FIGURE 13-1 INSIDER VERSUS OUTSIDER CEO PERFORMANCE

Despite a company's healthy or challenged state, insiders performed better.

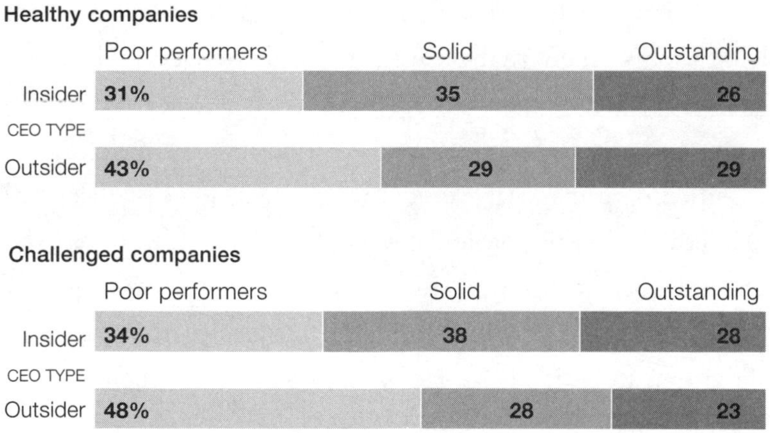

Healthy companies

CEO TYPE	Poor performers	Solid	Outstanding
Insider	31%	35	26
Outsider	43%	29	29

Challenged companies

CEO TYPE	Poor performers	Solid	Outstanding
Insider	34%	38	28
Outsider	48%	28	23

Note: A "healthy" company outperformed the market in the year prior to the CEO being hired. A "challenged" company underperformed the market in the year prior to the CEO being hired.
Source: Center for Talent Innovation

Of course, it is possible to find an outstanding protégé, invest your clout and your capital, and have these investments blow up in your face. For an example of spectacular failure—but eventual success—I'll turn to one of the most iconic businesspeople of our time: Steve Jobs.

Two Protégés—and Two Legacies

In 1983, Steve Jobs was rich and famous because of one product, the Apple II computer. But he was still a young man, and he knew that the Apple II wasn't enough for a legacy. He still wanted to make a "dent in the universe," as his biographer Walter Isaacson wrote.[3] At that time, IBM was beginning to dominate the personal computer market and to muscle out stiff competition from Apple, which in 1983 had just lost its president. The company needed someone to run it as it faced the transition from startup to corporate heavyweight. The Macintosh was still a work in progress, its success far from certain. Steve Jobs—then twenty-eight years old and with a habit of fostering fights among Apple employees, not resolving them—knew that he was "too rough-edged and immature" to be the steady hand on the wheel that Apple needed.[4] So he set out on a search for a CEO.

He settled on a marketing executive at Pepsi, John Sculley, and here something unusual began: it was often unclear who was the sponsor and who the protégé. After all, Jobs had hired Sculley—but Sculley was the older, more experienced businessperson, and Jobs had hired him to be his boss. He wanted Sculley to groom him to take the reins one day.

What is clear today is that both men went about the sponsor-protégé relationship in the wrong way. For a start, each was starstruck. "This has been one of the most exciting evenings of my whole life," Jobs said after one early meeting with Sculley. "I can learn so much from you." And: "You're the best person I've ever met." Sculley in turn said that he was "smitten" and "taken by this young, impetuous genius."[5]

Despite the enthusiasm, the two men failed to take the time to really get to know each other—to inspect the other's ability to deliver performance *and* loyalty. Once the initial infatuation faded, Jobs and Sculley found that they were incompatible men with incompatible ideas about where Apple should head.

The Protégé Who Betrays You

By 1985 it was clear that Sculley failed to share Jobs's passion for great design products. He was also failing to fill a gap in Jobs's skill set and add the value he'd been brought in for: effective, disciplined management. Macintosh, now launched, was selling poorly. IBM's domination of the home computer market was only growing.[6]

When the conflict between Sculley and Jobs became open, Apple's board of directors sided with Sculley and Jobs was soon out of the company he had cofounded. To deepen the betrayal, after Jobs left, the now Sculley-led Apple even sued him to try to force him to abandon his new venture.[7]

Sculley presided over a few good years, coasting off the company's earlier innovations. Then a steady decline in market share and profit began. The board eventually got rid of Sculley, but the decline continued. By 1996, Apple's market share of the personal computer market, which it had largely invented, was a mere 4 percent. It was losing $1 billion a year.[8]

Sculley, who was supposed to prepare Apple for lasting success and Jobs for leadership, had not only driven Jobs out of Apple; he had driven the company into an abyss.

The Protégé Who Perpetuates Your Vision

Jobs returned to Apple in 1997, first as a part-time adviser, then as CEO. The new products began flowing—the iMac, then the iPod and iPhone—and Apple was on its way to becoming what it is today: one of the most innovative, influential, and profitable companies in existence, with a brand considered the most valuable in the world.[9]

Jobs didn't do it alone. Aside from the brilliant engineers and designers, which Apple had never lacked, starting in 1998 Jobs had a man at his side who gave him performance and loyalty and filled in his gaps. This man—Tim Cook—is now, years after Jobs's death, still working to strengthen Jobs's legacy.

As Jobs told his biographer, Walter Isaacson, "So we [Cook and I] started to work together, and before long I trusted him to know exactly what to do . . . I could just forget about a lot of things unless he came and pinged me." Isaacson adds: "At Apple his [Cook's] role became implementing Jobs's intuition, which he accomplished with a quiet diligence."[10]

Note how different this beginning was from Jobs's beginning with Sculley. With Cook, Jobs didn't fall in love. He worked with him *before* deciding to trust him fully. And even then, Jobs was firmly in charge for many years after.

Cook gave not just loyalty. He also gave performance. With his background in procurement—Cook had been vice president for corporate materials at Compaq before coming to Apple—he cut Apple's inventory from two months to *two days*, slashed the production process per computer from four months to two, and cut the number of suppliers from one hundred to twenty-four. He also obliged suppliers to give Apple better deals than before. In many cases he also got them to locate next to Apple's plants—allowing him to shut nearly half the company's warehouses.[11]

All that was more than performance. It was doing what Jobs wasn't able to do himself. After all, visionaries don't always have steady hands on the wheel. Jobs was famously difficult—imperious, rude, and undisciplined, a perfectionist who often disrupted daily operations. Cook was calm and organized, a team player, the rational brain to Jobs's emotional fire.

He complemented Jobs's brilliant products and marketing campaigns by building a functioning company with streamlined operations, well-controlled costs, and an incomparable supply chain.

In 2011, Jobs, who'd been fighting pancreatic cancer for years, asked Cook to replace him as CEO. By then, the two men had grown so close that Cook had offered Jobs a portion of his liver, an offer Jobs refused.[12] Jobs died soon after.

Before he died, Jobs advised Cook to avoid second-guessing himself or asking, "What would Steve Jobs do?"[13] The fact that Jobs felt the need to say that was telling: he'd found a protégé whom he trusted so well to carry on his vision that he could urge him not to overdo it. Carrying on a sponsor's vision—just like being a good protégé while the sponsor is active—doesn't mean following their example blindly. It means bringing your intelligence and creativity to strengthen their ideas and eventually cement their legacy.

Cook has done that, as Apple romps from one milestone to the next, still innovating, still growing, still inspiring. And Cook is keeping Jobs's memory alive in other ways too. He talks about him often. "Steve's DNA will always be the core of Apple," he said in February 2017. "His philosophy will be at Apple 100 years from now."[14]

On Jobs's birthday last year, Cook went to Twitter to share memories of and quotes from Jobs.[15] When Apple opened a new thousand-seat auditorium, Cook naturally named it after Steve Jobs.[16] And in September 2017, when Cook hosted an event to celebrate the tenth anniversary of the iPhone, he opened it with a video of Jobs.[17]

That's what an immensely able and loyal protégé can do: help keep the organization, to which you've dedicated so much, growing and thriving long after you step down.

Keeping Legacy Alive—for a Century

There aren't many academics who change the world. There are even fewer who create a school of thought and remain influential in world affairs decades after their death.

One academic who did all that is John Maynard Keynes. And a central reason why he, unlike other brilliant economists, continues to have such influence is that he sponsored protégés, and his protégés in turn sponsored protégés.

In his lifetime, Keynes was a towering figure both in his profession and in global affairs. His 1919 book criticizing the Treaty of Versailles, *The Economic Consequences of the Peace*, helped shape global economic policy and international relations between the two world wars.

His work in the 1930s, especially his magnum opus, *The General Theory of Employment, Interest, and Money*, helped lead to the government programs that ended the Great Depression and were at the heart of economic policymaking after World War II. As the United Kingdom's representative to the Bretton Woods conference of 1944, Keynes helped create the global monetary and trade systems that defined the postwar world.

He died in 1946, but to this day, "Keynesian" economics remains a vital reference for government leaders worldwide. As an economist myself, I would argue that the brilliance of his ideas is the central reason why they became so important. But the traction they've gained over time is also due to the fact that Keynes cultivated protégés—who cultivate protégés too.

Lord John Eatwell, the Cambridge economics professor (and president of Queen's College) whom we met in chapter 10, explains that "Keynes looked after the people in his inner circle. He made sure that they got jobs at Cambridge."

Eatwell talks about two protégés of Keynes—Richard Kahn and Joan Robinson. Keynes helped get these two economists secure positions at Cambridge and they, in turn, contributed theoretical dimensions to the new Keynesian school of thought that emphasized "demand led" economic growth.

They also created a bridge to the next generation. Kahn and Robinson had their own protégés. Robinson advised Amartya Sen on his PhD thesis at Cambridge. Sen would go on to teach in Delhi, MIT, UC Berkeley, the London School of Economics, Harvard, and Oxford. He would also win the Nobel Prize. Another of Robinson's students, Manmohan Singh, became prime minister of India and led his country through the 2008 political crisis.[18] Given his Cambridge training and position as head of state, Singh was able to both formulate a Keynesian response to the crisis and ensure this approach was embedded in policy.[19]

For his part, Kahn brought the Italian economist Luigi Pasinetti as his protégé to Cambridge. Pasinetti became a much respected theorist, brilliant teacher and core member of the Cambridge faculty for decades. He took on his own protégés—one of whom, as we saw earlier, was John Eatwell.

In academia and in public life, Eatwell helped keep Keynesian ideas alive during the Thatcher–Reagan years when they were out of favor. He too has had his own protégés, who he helped secure positions Cambridge and Harvard. Since the 1990's he's been a leading spokesperson in the House of Lords for the United Kingdom's Labour Party.[20]

Due in part to Eatwell's efforts, there were many protégés of protégés of Keynes who, when the 2008 global financial crisis came around, could bring his ideas back to life. Alastair Darling, the UK chancellor of the exchequer during the crisis, said that his government's reaction at the time was "influenced hugely by Keynes's thinking, indeed, as were most other governments."[21]

That's how to maintain an influence in your field seventy years after your death: have protégés who in turn will have protégés and keep your legacy alive.

Coda

I chose to showcase famous examples of sponsor-protégé pairs in this legacy chapter because in different ways they represent examples of the highest levels to which one can aspire: growing and leading a world-class company and then successfully passing the baton; and founding a school of thought that cascades down through generations and shapes the global economy.

Some of this book's readers may be just at the start of their careers; and not everyone will aspire to lead a large enterprise or see their name become shorthand for a powerful brand of economic policymaking. But sponsorship, if done well, will enable you to rise higher than you might have otherwise, and it will help you leave a legacy behind. Whether you're at the middle ranks or the top, your best bet to leave your clients, your team, or your practice in good hands is to have a trusted protégé take over your responsibilities.

That's true whether you're retiring, or simply moving on to the next challenge—a new job, a new role in your company, even a new career. And if you are moving on to another challenge, odds are good that your former protégés will still be valuable friends and allies in the years and decades to come.

While a more robust legacy is the end point of this sponsorship journey, it's clearly not the sole point. The playbook outlined in this book provides a road map for all that comes before: enhanced professional success for yourself, a boost for the organization, and the satisfaction of knowing that you've helped deserving talent rise to the top.

Anyone who wants to make a difference in the world can find a payoff in aligning with standout junior talent. If you follow the playbook, your protégés will increase your bandwidth, have your back when you need it most, and provide skill sets that complement and fill out your own. Your protégés will thus turbocharge *your* progression, allowing you to go further and faster in your chosen field.

As a final word, let me reemphasize that sponsorship is about *reciprocity*. Although it rests on a quid pro quo and is transactional, at heart it is a mutually beneficial and generous relationship. Your protégés should gain enormously from the investments you make in them—and so should your organization.

Those are big rewards, and you'll need to make some serious commitments to earn them. Why not get started now?

Notes

Chapter 1

1. Mark Anthony Green, "Meet Maverick Carter, the Man Behind LeBron's Billion-Dollar Nike Deal," *GQ Style*, May 17, 2016, https://www.gq.com/story/lebron-james-nike-deal-bilion-maverick-carter.

2. Starting in 2010, the Center for Talent Innovation has spearheaded an extremely important body of work on the value of sponsorship. The arc of the research to date is as follows: "The Sponsor Effect: Breaking Through the Glass Ceiling" (*Harvard Business Review* research report, 2010); "The Relationship You Need to Get Right" (*Harvard Business Review* article, 2011); "Sponsor Effect: UK" (Center for Talent Innovation report, 2012); "Sponsor Effect 2.0" (Center for Talent Innovation report, 2012); "Vaulting the Color Bar" (Center for Talent Innovation report, 2013); *Forget a Mentor, Find a Sponsor* (Harvard Business Review Press book, 2014); *Growing Global Executives* (Center for Talent Innovation book, 2015); and "Sponsor Effect Canada" (Center for Talent Innovation report, 2016).

    The survey underlying this book was fielded by NORC at the University of Chicago. It was conducted online and over the phone in January 2018 among 3,213 respondents (half men half women) between the ages of 21 and 65, who were currently employed in white-collar occupations and had at least a bachelor's degree. Data is weighted to be representative of the US population on key demographics (age, sex, education, race/ethnicity, etc.).

3. Sylvia Ann Hewlett, with Kerrie Peraino, Laura Sherbin, and Karen Sumberg, "The Sponsor Effect: Breaking Through the Last Glass Ceiling," *Harvard Business Review* research report, December 2010.

4. Steve Goldstein, "Sheryl Sandberg Leans In for Larry Summers," MarketWatch, July 31, 2013, http://blogs.marketwatch.com/capitolreport/2013/07/31/sheryl-sandberg-leans-in-for-larry-summers/; Sheryl Sandberg, "Larry Summers' True Record on Women," *Huffington Post*, May 25, 2011, https://www.huffingtonpost.com/sheryl-sandberg/what-larry-summers-has-do_b_142126.html.

5. Peter Fearon, "Condi Now: The Cost of Loyalty," Newser, September 3, 2007, http://www.newser.com/story/6844/condi-now-the-cost-of-loyalty.html.

6. Dana Hughes, "Georg W. Bush's Legacy on Africa Wins Praise, Even from Foes," ABC News, April 26, 2013, http://abcnews.go.com/blogs/politics/2013/04/george-w-bushs-legacy-on-africa-wins-praise-even-from-foes/.

Chapter 2

1. United States Department of Education, "Bachelor's, Master's, and Doctor's Degrees Conferred by Postsecondary Institutions, by Sex of Student and Discipline Division: 2013–14," Institute of Education Sciences, National Center for Education Statistics, https://nces.ed.gov/programs/digest/d15/tables/dt15_318.30.asp?current=yes; United States Department of Education, "Bachelor's Degrees Conferred by Postsecondary Institutions, by Race/Ethnicity and Sex of Student: Selected Years, 1976–77 through 2014–15," Institute of Education Sciences, National Center for Education Statistics, https://nces.ed.gov/programs/digest/d16/tables/dt16_322.20.asp?current=yes; United States Department of Education, "Master's Degrees Conferred by Postsecondary Institutions, by Race/Ethnicity and Sex of Student: Selected Years, 1976–77 through 2014–15," Institute of Education Sciences, National Center for Education Statistics, https://nces.ed.gov/programs/digest/d16/tables/dt16_323.20.asp?current=yes; United States Department of Education, "Doctor's Degrees Conferred by Postsecondary Institutions, by Race/Ethnicity and Sex of Student: Selected Years, 1976–77 through 2014–15," Institute of Education Sciences, National Center for Education Statistics, https://nces.ed.gov/programs/digest/d16/tables/dt16_324.20.asp?current=yes.

2. Equal Employment Opportunity Commission, "2015 Job Patterns for Minorities and Women in Private Industry (EEO-1)," US Equal Employment Opportunity Commission, https://www1.eeoc.gov/eeoc/statistics/employment/jobpat-eeo1/2015/index.cfm#select_label.

3. Valentina Zarya, "Female *Fortune* 500 CEOs Are Poised to Break This Record in 2017," *Fortune*, December 22, 2016, http://fortune.com/2016/12/22/female-fortune-500-ceos-2017/; "Black *Fortune* 500 CEOs Decline by 33%," Diversity Inc., June 30, 2015, http://bestpractices.diversityinc.com/talent-management/shortfalls-and-bias-driven-discrepancies-war-for-talent/black-fortune-500-ceos-decline-by-33-in-past-year/.

4. Sylvia Ann Hewlett, with Kerrie Peraino, Laura Sherbin, and Karen Sumberg, "The Sponsor Effect: Breaking Through the Last Glass Ceiling," *Harvard Business Review* research report, December 2010.

5. Sylvia Ann Hewlett, Melinda Marshall, and Laura Sherbin, *Sponsor Effect 2.0: Road Maps for Sponsors and Protégés* (New York: Center for Talent Innovation, 2012).

6. "The Sponsor Effect."

7. "The Sponsor Effect"; *Sponsor Effect 2.0*; Sylvia Ann Hewlett and Ripa Rashid, *Growing Global Executives: The New Competencies* (New York: Center for Talent Innovation, 2015); Sylvia Ann Hewlett, Todd Sears, Karen Sumberg, and Christina Fargnoli, *The Power of "Out" 2.0: LGBT in the Workplace* (New York, Center for Talent Innovation, 2013).

8. Unpublished data from Hewlett, *Sponsor Effect 2.0*.

Chapter 3

1. Name anonymized at Tiger Tyagarajan's request.
2. Sheelah Kolhatkar, "Mayor Bloomberg's Delicate Condition," *Entrepreneur*, December 8, 2008, https://www.entrepreneur.com/article/199110.

Chapter 5

1. Tom Kludt, "News Anchor Joins Lawsuit Alleging Racial Discrimination, Harassment at Network," CNN Business, April 26, 2017, http://money.cnn .com/2017/04/25/media/fox-news-racial-discrimination-lawsuit/index.html.
2. Jordan Bryan, "Connector Managers Drive Service Rep Productivity," Gartner, October 24, 2018, https://www.cebglobal.com/blogs/corporate-hr-how-genpact-retains-new-mothers-on-its-workforce/; Saumya Bhattacharya, "Career 2.0: Genpact Gives Women on Break a Chance to Comeback," *Economic Times*, July 7, 2015, https://economictimes.indiatimes.com/jobs/career-2-0-genpact-gives-women-on-break-a-chance-to-comeback/articleshow/47965854.cms; Shubhra Rishi, "How Genpact Is Addressing the Gender Imbalance in Their IT Workforce," *CIO & Leader*, February 28, 2017, http://www.cioandleader.com/article/2017/02/28/how-genpact-addressing-gender-imbalance-their-it-workforce.
3. Sylvia Ann Hewlett, Melinda Marshall, and Laura Sherbin, with Tara Gonsalves, *Innovation, Diversity, and Market Growth* (New York: Center for Talent Innovation, 2013).

Chapter 7

1. Sylvia Ann Hewlett, Melinda Marshall, and Laura Sherbin, with Tara Gonsalves, *Innovation, Diversity, and Market Growth* (New York: Center for Talent Innovation, 2013).

Chapter 9

1. Nicholas Fandos and Maggie Haberman, "Ronny Jackson, Failed V.A. Pick, Is Unlikely to Return as Trump's Doctor," *New York Times*, April 29, 2018, https://www.nytimes.com/2018/04/29/us/politics/ronny-jackson-trump-white-house.html.

Chapter 10

1. "Working Mother Names #1 Best Company for Moms: Unilever," AP News, September 25, 2018, https://apnews.com/15bc42aa583244178538e5af0 a39d8e5.

Chapter 12

1. Center for Talent Innovation, *What #MeToo Means for Corporate America* (New York, 2018), 14–15.

2. Ibid., 26.

3. *What #MeToo Means for Corporate America.*

4. Brandon N. Cline, Ralph A. Walkling, and Adam S. Yore, "The Consequences of Indiscretions: Sex, Lies, and Firm Value," *Journal of Financial Economics* (forthcoming), https://papers.ssrn.com/sol3/papers .cfm?abstract_id=1573327.

5. Julie Creswell, Kevin Draper, and Rachel Abrams, "At Nike, Revolt Led by Women Leads to Exodus of Male Executives," *New York Times*, April 28, 2018, https://www.nytimes.com/2018/04/28/business/nike-women.html.

6. *What #MeToo Means for Corporate America*, 55.

7. Claire Cain Miller, "Unintended Consequences of Sexual Harassment Scandals," *New York Times,* October 9, 2017, https://www.nytimes.com/ 2017/10/09/upshot/as-sexual-harassment-scandals-spook-men-it-can-backfire-for-women.html?_r=0.

8. Ibid.

9. Sylvia Ann Hewlett, Melinda Marshall, and Laura Sherbin, with Tara Gonsalves, *Innovation, Diversity, and Market Growth* (New York: Center for Talent Innovation, 2013), 19.

10. Andrea Turner Moffett, *Harness the Power of the Purse* (Los Angeles: Rare Bird Books, 2015).

11. Peter Beaumont, "The Sphinx," *Guardian*, April 3, 2004, https://www .theguardian.com/world/2004/apr/04/september11.usa; Paul Harris, "How Condoleezza Rice Became the Most Powerful Woman in the World," *Guardian*, January 15, 2005, https://www.theguardian.com/world/2005/jan/16/usa .paulharris1; Sheryl Gay Stolberg, "Dinner with Rice," *New York Times*, January 18, 2009, https://thecaucus.blogs.nytimes.com/2009/01/18/dinner-with-rice/.

12. Ian Ayres and Cait Unkovic, "Information Escrows," *University of Michigan Law Review* 111, no. 2 (2012); Daniel Zielinski, "Apps Bypass HR to Send Harassment Reports Directly to Senior Leaders," Society for Human Resource Management, February 12, 2018, https://www.shrm.org/resourcesandtools/hr-topics/technology/pages/apps-bypass-hr-to-send-harassment-reports-directly-to-senior-leaders.aspx.

Chapter 13

1. Spencer Stuart, "Select Insights from the 2017 Spencer Stuart S&P 500 CEO Study," April 2017.

2. Ibid.

3. Walter Isaacson, *Steve Jobs* (New York: Simon and Schuster, 2011), 92.

4. Ibid., 148.

5. Ibid., 150–153.

6. Ibid., 194–195.

7. Ibid., 217.

8. Ibid., 296.

9. Kurt Badenhausen, "Apple Heads the World's Most Valuable Brands of 2017 at $170 Billion," *Forbes*, May 23, 2017, https://www.forbes.com/sites/kurtbadenhausen/2017/05/23/apple-heads-the-worlds-most-valuable-brands-of-2017-at-170-billion.

10. Isaacson, 359–360.

11. Ibid.

12. "Steve Jobs Rejected Liver Transplant Offer from Tim Cook," *Guardian*, March 13, 2015, https://www.theguardian.com/technology/2015/mar/13/steve-jobs-rejected-liver-transplant-offer-from-tim-cook.

13. Daisuke Wakabayashi, "Tim Cook's Vision for 'His' Apple Begins to Emerge," *Wall Street Journal*, July 7, 2014, https://www.wsj.com/articles/tim-cooks-apple-takes-shape-1404757939.

14. Arjun Kharpal, "Apple's Tim Cook: Steve Jobs' Philosophy Will Be at Apple in 100 Years," CNBC.com, February 9, 2017, https://www.cnbc.com/2017/02/09/apple-ceo-tim-cook-steve-jobs-philosophy-will-be-at-apple-in-100-years.html.

15. Jonathan Vanian, "Apple CEO Tim Cook Shares Words of Wisdom from Steve Jobs," *Fortune*, February 24, 2017, http://fortune.com/2017/02/24/apple-ceo-tim-cook-steve-jobs/.

16. Mike Wuerthele, "Apple Park's Campus Auditorium Named 'Steve Jobs Theater,' Opens Later in the Year," AppleInsider, February 22, 2017, http://appleinsider.com/articles/17/02/22/apple-parks-campus-auditorium-named-steve-jobs-theater-opens-later-in-year.

17. Jena McGregor, "Steve Jobs Still Looms Large at Apple. Tim Cook Seems Just Fine with That," *Washington Post*, September 13, 2017, https://www.washingtonpost.com/news/on-leadership/wp/2017/09/13/steve-jobs-still-loomed-large-at-apples-big-event-tim-cook-seems-just-fine-with-that/?utm_term=.9342efbc62d3.

18. Mark Tully, "Architect of the New India," *Cambridge Alumni Magazine*, Michaelmas 2005.

19. Manmohan Singh, speech at G20 Meeting, *Hindustan Times*, November 16, 2008, https://www.hindustantimes.com/business/manmohan-singh-s-speech-at-g20-meet/story-CSEJcziMIepsfELSKrcleO.html.

20. "Labour's New Front Bench Team," Labour website, https://web.archive.org/web/20110809174053/http://www2.labour.org.uk/labours-new-front-bench-team.

21. Alistair Darling, *Back from the Brink: 1,000 Days at Number 11* (London: Atlantic Books, 2011), 177.

Index

Acknowledgments

This book is especially significant to me. It brings together ten years of research and writing on the power of sponsorship to fast-track careers across the lines of difference (gender, race, and culture, but also fields of expertise). It was also written during a year I faced significant health challenges. It therefore gives me great pleasure to thank those who lifted me up and pulled me through: my magnificent family (husband, children, and grandchildren) who were ever-ready with great gobs of generous love; close-in friends who showed up, buoyed my spirits, and pitched in. And my surgical team at Memorial Sloan Kettering, whose skills, judgment, and wisdom turned my prospects around.

I have other important debts of gratitude:

- To Dan Horch and Nell Casey, whose editorial skills contributed enormously to this book.

- To CTI's board, executive leadership, and world-class research team.

- To the forty-plus senior executives who spent precious hours in one-on-one interviews, sharing—at a granular level—the tools and tactics they use to maximize sponsorship payoff. Their honest, eloquent voices thread through this book.

- To HBR's extraordinary editorial team, particularly Melinda Merino, Courtney Cashman, and Jennifer Waring. This is the

fifth book I've written with HBR, and it could not have been a
better experience.

- To Robert Levinson and Helen Churko, my speaking agents at
  Royce Carlton, who are making sure that the powerful playbook at the heart of this book spreads far and wide.

About the Author

Sylvia Ann Hewlett is an economist and the CEO of Hewlett Consulting Partners. She is also the founder and Chair Emeritus of the Center for Talent Innovation. The author of fourteen critically acclaimed books, including *Winning the War for Talent in Emerging Markets; Forget a Mentor, Find a Sponsor* (an Audible bestseller); and *Executive Presence* (an Amazon "Best Book of the Month"), she has appeared on *60 Minutes, Morning Joe,* the *Today Show*—and has been lampooned on *Saturday Night Live.* Hewlett has taught at Cambridge, Columbia, and Princeton universities and earned her PhD in economics at London University.